IN ASSOCIATION WITH SQA

Hodder Gibson Model Practice Papers WITH ANSWERS

PLUS: Official SQA Specimen Paper With Answers

Higher for CfE
German

2014 Specimen Question Paper & Model Papers

Hodder Gibson Study Skills Advice – General	– page 3
Hodder Gibson Study Skills Advice – Higher for CfE German	– page 5
2014 SPECIMEN QUESTION PAPER	– page 9
MODEL PAPER 1	– page 35
MODEL PAPER 2	– page 61
MODEL PAPER 3	– page 87
MODEL PAPER 4	– page 113
ANSWER SECTION	– page 139

HODDER GIBSON
AN HACHETTE UK COMPANY

This book contains the official 2014 SQA Specimen Question Paper for Higher for CfE German, with associated SQA approved answers modified from the official marking instructions that accompany the paper.

In addition the book contains model practice papers, together with answers, plus study skills advice. These papers, some of which may include a limited number of previously published SQA questions, have been specially commissioned by Hodder Gibson, and have been written by experienced senior teachers and examiners in line with the new Higher for CfE syllabus and assessment outlines, Spring 2014. This is not SQA material but has been devised to provide further practice for Higher for CfE examinations in 2015 and beyond.

Hodder Gibson is grateful to the copyright holders, as credited on the final page of the Answer Section, for permission to use their material. Every effort has been made to trace the copyright holders and to obtain their permission for the use of copyright material. Hodder Gibson will be happy to receive information allowing us to rectify any error or omission in future editions.

Hachette UK's policy is to use papers that are natural, renewable and recyclable products and made from wood grown in sustainable forests. The logging and manufacturing processes are expected to conform to the environmental regulations of the country of origin.

Orders: please contact Bookpoint Ltd, 130 Park Drive, Abingdon, Oxon OX14 4SE. Telephone: (44) 01235 827720. Fax: (44) 01235 400454. Lines are open 9.00–5.00, Monday to Saturday, with a 24-hour message answering service. Visit our website at www.hoddereducation.co.uk. Hodder Gibson can be contacted direct on: Tel: 0141 848 1609; Fax: 0141 889 6315; email: hoddergibson@hodder.co.uk

This collection first published in 2015 by
Hodder Gibson, an imprint of Hodder Education,
An Hachette UK Company
2a Christie Street
Paisley PA1 1NB

BrightRED Hodder Gibson is grateful to Bright Red Publishing Ltd for collaborative work in preparation of this book and all SQA Past Paper, National 5 and Higher for CfE Model Paper titles 2014.

Specimen Question Paper © Scottish Qualifications Authority. Answers, Model Question Papers, and Study Skills Section © Hodder Gibson. Model Question Papers creation/compilation, Answers and Study Skills section © Hodder Gibson. All rights reserved. Apart from any use permitted under UK copyright law, no part of this publication may be reproduced or transmitted in any form or by any means, electronic or mechanical, including photocopying and recording, or held within any information storage and retrieval system, without permission in writing from the publisher or under licence from the Copyright Licensing Agency Limited. Further details of such licences (for reprographic reproduction) may be obtained from the Copyright Licensing Agency Limited, Saffron House, 6–10 Kirby Street, London EC1N 8TS.

Typeset by PDQ Digital Media Solutions Ltd, Bungay, Suffolk NR35 1BY

Printed in the UK

A catalogue record for this title is available from the British Library

ISBN: 978-1-4718-4000-5

3 2 1

2016 2015

Introduction

Study Skills – what you need to know to pass exams!

Pause for thought

Many students might skip quickly through a page like this. After all, we all know how to revise. Do you really though?

Think about this:

"IF YOU ALWAYS DO WHAT YOU ALWAYS DO, YOU WILL ALWAYS GET WHAT YOU HAVE ALWAYS GOT."

Do you like the grades you get? Do you want to do better? If you get full marks in your assessment, then that's great! Change nothing! This section is just to help you get that little bit better than you already are.

There are two main parts to the advice on offer here. The first part highlights fairly obvious things but which are also very important. The second part makes suggestions about revision that you might not have thought about but which WILL help you.

Part 1

DOH! It's so obvious but …

Start revising in good time

Don't leave it until the last minute – this will make you panic.

Make a revision timetable that sets out work time AND play time.

Sleep and eat!

Obvious really, and very helpful. Avoid arguments or stressful things too – even games that wind you up. You need to be fit, awake and focused!

Know your place!

Make sure you know exactly **WHEN and WHERE** your exams are.

Know your enemy!

Make sure you know what to expect in the exam.

How is the paper structured?

How much time is there for each question?

What types of question are involved?

Which topics seem to come up time and time again?

Which topics are your strongest and which are your weakest?

Are all topics compulsory or are there choices?

Learn by DOING!

There is no substitute for past papers and practice papers – they are simply essential! Tackling this collection of papers and answers is exactly the right thing to be doing as your exams approach.

Part 2

People learn in different ways. Some like low light, some bright. Some like early morning, some like evening/night. Some prefer warm, some prefer cold. But everyone uses their BRAIN and the brain works when it is active. Passive learning – sitting gazing at notes – is the most INEFFICIENT way to learn anything. Below you will find tips and ideas for making your revision more effective and maybe even more enjoyable. What follows gets your brain active, and active learning works!

Activity 1 – Stop and review

Step 1

When you have done no more than 5 minutes of revision reading STOP!

Step 2

Write a heading in your own words which sums up the topic you have been revising.

Step 3

Write a summary of what you have revised in no more than two sentences. Don't fool yourself by saying, "I know it, but I cannot put it into words". That just means you don't know it well enough. If you cannot write your summary, revise that section again, knowing that you must write a summary at the end of it. Many of you will have notebooks full of blue/black ink writing. Many of the pages will not be especially attractive or memorable so try to liven them up a bit with colour as you are reviewing and rewriting. **This is a great memory aid, and memory is the most important thing.**

Activity 2 — Use technology!

Why should everything be written down? Have you thought about "mental" maps, diagrams, cartoons and colour to help you learn? And rather than write down notes, why not record your revision material?

What about having a text message revision session with friends? Keep in touch with them to find out how and what they are revising and share ideas and questions.

Why not make a video diary where you tell the camera what you are doing, what you think you have learned and what you still have to do? No one has to see or hear it, but the process of having to organise your thoughts in a formal way to explain something is a very important learning practice.

Be sure to make use of electronic files. You could begin to summarise your class notes. Your typing might be slow, but it will get faster and the typed notes will be easier to read than the scribbles in your class notes. Try to add different fonts and colours to make your work stand out. You can easily Google relevant pictures, cartoons and diagrams which you can copy and paste to make your work more attractive and **MEMORABLE**.

Activity 3 – This is it. Do this and you will know lots!

Step 1

In this task you must be very honest with yourself! Find the SQA syllabus for your subject (www.sqa.org.uk). Look at how it is broken down into main topics called MANDATORY knowledge. That means stuff you MUST know.

Step 2

BEFORE you do ANY revision on this topic, write a list of everything that you already know about the subject. It might be quite a long list but you only need to write it once. It shows you all the information that is already in your long-term memory so you know what parts you do not need to revise!

Step 3

Pick a chapter or section from your book or revision notes. Choose a fairly large section or a whole chapter to get the most out of this activity.

With a buddy, use Skype, Facetime, Twitter or any other communication you have, to play the game "If this is the answer, what is the question?". For example, if you are revising Geography and the answer you provide is "meander", your buddy would have to make up a question like "What is the word that describes a feature of a river where it flows slowly and bends often from side to side?".

Make up 10 "answers" based on the content of the chapter or section you are using. Give this to your buddy to solve while you solve theirs.

Step 4

Construct a wordsearch of at least 10 X 10 squares. You can make it as big as you like but keep it realistic. Work together with a group of friends. Many apps allow you to make wordsearch puzzles online. The words and phrases can go in any direction and phrases can be split. Your puzzle must only contain facts linked to the topic you are revising. Your task is to find 10 bits of information to hide in your puzzle, but you must not repeat information that you used in Step 3. DO NOT show where the words are. Fill up empty squares with random letters. Remember to keep a note of where your answers are hidden but do not show your friends. When you have a complete puzzle, exchange it with a friend to solve each other's puzzle.

Step 5

Now make up 10 questions (not "answers" this time) based on the same chapter used in the previous two tasks. Again, you must find NEW information that you have not yet used. Now it's getting hard to find that new information! Again, give your questions to a friend to answer.

Step 6

As you have been doing the puzzles, your brain has been actively searching for new information. Now write a NEW LIST that contains only the new information you have discovered when doing the puzzles. Your new list is the one to look at repeatedly for short bursts over the next few days. Try to remember more and more of it without looking at it. After a few days, you should be able to add words from your second list to your first list as you increase the information in your long-term memory.

FINALLY! Be inspired...

Make a list of different revision ideas and beside each one write **THINGS I HAVE** tried, **THINGS I WILL** try and **THINGS I MIGHT** try. Don't be scared of trying something new.

And remember – "FAIL TO PREPARE AND PREPARE TO FAIL!"

After you have read the text:
- Read the comprehension questions carefully.
- Underline the question word and circle the number of points to highlight what information and how many points the examiner is looking for.
- Make sure that you give as much detail as possible – again look at the number of marks. At CfE Higher, the examiner is looking for detailed answers so check before and after your answer in the text to see if you have missed anything.
- Do not give alternatives – commit to your answer.
- Remember that the translation will **not** contain an answer to the comprehension questions – skim over it to save time.

When working on the translation section:
- Only attempt the translation after having read the text.
- Ensure that you accurately translate the words – watch out for separable verbs!
- Know what tense your verbs are in.
- Make sure you convey the meaning in good English.
- Do **NOT** miss out any words.

After you have answered the questions:
- Check your answers – read the question first and then your response – does it answer the question?
- Make sure that your answers in English make sense and your English is of a good standard.

Directed Writing tips

Before you sit your Directed Writing exam:
- Make sure you are familiar with the *Perfekt* and *Imperfekt* tenses.
- Practise writing different types of scenarios.
- Prepare a bank of phrases which you can use to impress the examiner.
- Read through the whole scenario carefully.
- Plan and structure your essay – leave enough time to check it.

During the Directed Writing exam:
- Write legibly so that the examiner can read what you've written.
- Set the scene – give an introduction of where you went and how you got there (even if it's not a bullet point!)
- Tick off the bullet points as you complete them.
- Ensure you convey the scenario accurately.
- Restrict your use of the dictionary to looking up keywords required to convey the message in the scenario and to check spelling and genders of what you have already written.
- Avoid translating from English to German – you will end up using English grammar.
- Remember you are encouraged to give any other details – so feel free to add any of those phrases you have prepared.
- Time yourself – try and restrict the time spent writing to 40 minutes.

After you have finished writing:
- Check you have covered all the bullet points (some bullet points have more than one part!)
- Go back through and check your grammar and spelling:
    - does your *Perfekt* construction have a subject, auxiliary verb and a past participle? e.g. Ich habe gesehen, ich bin geflogen
    - have you used the correct form *sein/haben* with your *Perfekt* construction?
    - check the genders of nouns
    - agreements – verbs and adjectives
    - cases – dative or accusative?
    - do all the nouns have capital letters?
- Check that your writing makes sense!

Listening tips

It is important that you regularly learn your vocabulary so that you are able to recognise words and phrases. Develop a system to help you do this: make flashcards, use vocabulary apps on your smartphone or online, use internet sites such as *Youtube* to listen to contemporary German, or even ask a family member to test you.

Before you sit your Listening exam:
- Revise vocabulary, especially verbs in different tense forms, quantifiers (viel, wenig, die meisten), numbers and dates. Read vocabulary out loud so that you can recognise how it sounds.
- Read the introduction and think about what you know about the topic.
- Remember to listen for cognates and near-cognates.
- Remember that practice makes perfect.
- Read the questions in English carefully – you are given time to study them before the text starts – underline question words and anticipate what type of answers you are listening for.
- Remember that the questions come in the same order as the text.

While you are sitting your Listening exam:
- You will hear both items (monologue and dialogue) twice so you don't need to get all the details on the first go.
- Make sure the examiner can see your final answer.
- If you don't understand a word, you need to use the context to help work it out or find a logical answer.
- Look at how many marks are allocated to the question – this will guide how much you need to write.
- Try to give as much detail as possible.

After your Listening exam:
- Look over your answers – make sure what you've written in English makes sense.
- Use a single line to strike through notes or draft answers.

Essay writing tips for the short essay

Before you sit your Writing exam:
- Practise writing short essays after each topic.
- Prepare a bank of killer phrases.
- Read through the whole question carefully.
- Plan and structure your essay and leave enough time to check it.

During the Writing exam:
- Write legibly so that the examiner can read what you've written.
- Write an introduction.
- Tick off the questions as you complete them.
- Use essay phrases and connectors to make your writing more interesting.
- Ensure you convey the scenario accurately.
- Restrict your use of the dictionary to looking up keywords and to checking spelling and genders of what you have already written.
- Avoid translating from English to German – you will end up using English grammar.
- Pace yourself – you only have 30 minutes!

After you have finished writing:
- Check you have answered all the questions.
- Go back through and check your grammar and spelling:
    - verb endings
    - check the genders of nouns
    - agreements – verbs and adjectives
    - cases – dative or accusative?
    - do all the nouns have capital letters?
- Check that your writing makes sense!

Good luck!

Remember that the rewards for passing CfE Higher German are well worth it! Your pass will help you get the future you want for yourself. In the exam, be confident in your own ability. If you're not sure how to answer a question, trust your instincts and just give it a go anyway – keep calm and don't panic! GOOD LUCK!

HIGHER FOR CfE

2014 Specimen Question Paper

SQ21/H/11

German Reading

Date — Not applicable

Duration — 1 hour and 40 minutes

Total marks — 30

Attempt ALL questions.

Write your answers clearly, in **English**, in the Reading Answer Booklet provided. In the answer booklet you must clearly identify the question number you are attempting.

You may use a German dictionary.

Use **blue** or **black** ink.

There is a separate question and answer booklet for Directed Writing. You must complete your answer for Directed Writing in the question and answer booklet for Directed Writing.

Before leaving the examination room you must give your Reading answer booklet and your Directed Writing answer booklet to the Invigilator; if you do not, you may lose all the marks for this paper.

Total marks — 30

Attempt ALL questions

Read the whole article carefully and then answer, in English, ALL the questions that follow.

The article discusses the use of digital media in German schools.

Digitale Medien in der Schule - Vorteil oder Nachteil?

In den heutigen Schulen ist der PC mehr und mehr ein Lerninstrument im Klassenzimmer. Smartphones, Notebooks und Tablet-Computer gehören heute zum Alltag von Jugendlichen in Deutschland – und spielen auch eine wichtige Rolle beim Lernen. Aber helfen digitale Medien den Schülern wirklich bei der Vorbereitung auf die Zukunft?

5 Karl-Otto Kirst, ein Geschichtslehrer aus Hamburg, beschreibt, wie die digitalen Medien seinen Unterricht verändert haben: „Vor zehn Jahren, wenn ich meinen Schülern einen Film zeigen wollte, war das immer sehr aufwendig. Wir mussten entweder im Klassenzimmer die gesamte Technik aufbauen oder gleich in den Computerraum gehen. Heute haben wir einen Projektor und eine elektronische Tafel im Klassenzimmer und die
10 Filmpräsentation ist nur wenige Klicks entfernt."

Moderne Medien haben viele Vorteile, aber ihr Nutzen im Klassenzimmer ist umstritten - besonders seit der Arzt Dr. Manfred Spitzer in seinem Bestseller „Digitale Demenz" moderne Medien kritisiert hat. Dr. Spitzer ist der Meinung, dass Smartphones und Computer Kinder passiv machen können. Er warnt vor einer zu intensiven Benutzung von
15 elektronischen Medien im Klassenzimmer, weil das zu einer sehr oberflächlichen Beschäftigung mit Informationen führt. Er meint, dass Computer die Schüler süchtig machen.

Dr. Spitzer ist nicht der einzige, der sich Sorgen macht. Viele Lehrer und Lehrerinnen sowie Bildungspolitiker sind sehr kritisch, wenn es um den Einsatz neuer Medien in der
20 Schule geht. Ihrer Meinung nach ist die Mediennutzung häufig zeitraubend, weil die Lehrer technische Probleme haben. Oft geht es beim Einsatz neuer Medien mehr um die schöne Form als um den Inhalt. Die Schüler machen bessere Fortschritte, wenn sie aktiv lernen. Auch Eltern bezweifeln die Vorteile neuer Medien; sie fordern eine Rückbesinnung auf Tafel, Kreide und Bücher.

25 Heike Bühler, die bald ihr Abitur in einem Heidelberger Gymnasium macht, ist der Meinung, dass moderne Technik in vielen Klassenzimmern fehlt. „Die Schulen, die ich kenne, sind digital unterschiedlich ausgerüstet. Bei uns im Gymnasium ist es nicht schlecht, doch andere Gymnasien, wo ich Freunde habe, wie auch die meisten Haupt-und Realschulen können es sich finanziell nicht leisten, immer die neusten Geräte zu kaufen."

30 Auf dieses Problem deutet Christian Spannagel, Professor in Heidelberg, hin: „Deutschland ist die stärkste Wirtschaftsnation in Europa – aber die mangelhafte digitale Ausstattung von Schulen ist ein Schwachpunkt in der bundesdeutschen Bildungspolitik."

Laut einer Umfrage von Deutsche Telekom beurteilen nur vier Prozent der befragten Eltern in Deutschland den Einsatz von Computern in Schulen als ausgezeichnet. Nur in
35 einer von zehn Schulen hat jeder Schüler im Unterricht Zugang zu einem Computer. Und nur bei jedem dritten Schüler kommt der Computer mindestens einmal pro Woche im Unterricht zum Einsatz. Bei 30 Prozent wird der Computer im Unterricht überhaupt nicht benutzt.

Professor Spannagel ist überzeugt, dass dieses Problem erst dann gelöst wird, wenn die
40 Schüler ihre eigenen Geräte mitbringen dürfen. Aber nicht alle Schulen erlauben den Schülern ihre Handys als Lerninstrumente zu benutzen. In einigen Schulen gibt es eine Regel in der Schulordnung, die sagt, dass Handys und Smartphones im Unterricht

ausgeschaltet sein müssen. Man kann aber eine Ausnahme machen, wenn der Lehrer die Benutzung ausdrücklich erlaubt.

45 Im Allgemeinen sind die Umfrageergebnisse für Lehrer nicht sehr gut. Etwa die Hälfte aller Schüler bewertet die Medienkompetenz von Lehrern als negativ. Jeder dritte Schüler bezeichnet die Computerkenntnisse ihrer Lehrer als „mangelhaft". Die meisten Lehrer nutzen die Hard- und Software nur, um Filme oder Präsentationen zu zeigen. Die Produktion von Hörspielen, Podcasts oder Filmen zu Unterrichtsthemen bleibt noch die
50 Ausnahme.

Professor Spannagel erklärt, dass Lehrer oft unsicher und ängstlich im Umgang mit der neuen Technik sind. Lehrer haben einen stressigen Alltag und deshalb kaum Zeit, auf dem neusten Stand der aktuellen Medienentwicklung zu bleiben. Er glaubt, dass eine andere Haltung nötig ist. Lehrer brauchen mehr Experimentierfreude und sollten weniger Angst
55 haben, Fehler zu machen, damit digitale Medien mehr und mehr als Lerninstrument an deutschen Schulen zu finden sind.

MARKS

Questions

Re-read lines 1—10

1. According to the text, why is technology increasingly present in schools nowadays? State **two** things.   2

2. Karl-Otto Kirst explains how digital media have changed his lessons over the last ten years. What has changed? Give any **three** details.   3

Re-read lines 11—24

3. According to Dr Spitzer's research, what impact can the use of smartphones and computers have on children? State any **two** things.   2

4. What criticism do many teachers and politicians make of new media in schools? Give any **two** details.   2

Re-read lines 25—44

5. Heike Bühler states that many German classrooms lack technology. What does she know from her own experience? Give **three** details.   3

6. According to a survey by Deutsche Telekom, what evidence is there that German pupils are not getting enough access to computers in their schools? Give any **three** details.   3

7. What does Professor Spannagel suggest to overcome this lack of technology in schools? State **one** thing.   1

Re-read lines 51–56

MARKS

8. What reasons does Professor Spannagel give for some teachers' lack of confidence about the new media? State **two** things. **2**

9. Now consider the article as a whole. Does the writer give a positive or a negative view of the use of digital media in German classrooms? Give reasons for your answer with reference to the text. **2**

10. Translate into English:

    "Im Allgemeinen .... zu zeigen." (*lines 45–48*) **10**

[END OF SPECIMEN QUESTION PAPER]

H

National Qualifications
SPECIMEN ONLY

FOR OFFICIAL USE

Mark

SQ21/H/02

German
Directed Writing

Date — Not applicable

Duration — 1 hour and 40 minutes

Fill in these boxes and read what is printed below.

Full name of centre

Town

Forename(s)

Surname

Number of seat

Date of birth

Day   Month   Year

Scottish candidate number

Total marks — 10

Choose ONE scenario on *Page two* and write your answer clearly, in **German**, in the space provided in this booklet. You must clearly identify the scenario number you are attempting.

You may use a German dictionary.

Additional space for answers is provided at the end of this booklet.

Use **blue** or **black** ink.

There is a separate answer booklet for Reading. You must complete your answers for Reading in the answer booklet for Reading.

Before leaving the examination room you must give this Directed Writing question and answer booklet and your Reading answer booklet to the Invigilator; if you do not, you may lose all the marks for this paper.

Total marks — 10

Choose **one** of the following two scenarios.

SCENARIO 1: Employability

> You have been working in a café in Germany to develop your language skills and gain work experience.
>
> You write a short article in German about your experiences there for the local newspaper.

You must include the following information and **you should try to add** other relevant details:

- where you found the job advert **and** how you applied for the job
- what kind of work you have been doing
- what you thought about the job
- whether you would recommend a summer job abroad

You should write approximately 120–150 words.

OR

SCENARIO 2: Culture

> On your return from a gap year abroad, you write an article in German for the Modern Languages Department website of your school/college.

You must include the following information and **you should try to add** other relevant details:

- where you went **and** why you went there
- how you funded your gap year
- what you learned about the country
- whether you would recommend a gap year

You should write approximately 120–150 words.

Scenario number ☐

ANSWER SPACE (continued)

ANSWER SPACE (continued)

ADDITIONAL SPACE FOR ANSWERS

ADDITIONAL SPACE FOR ANSWERS

H

National Qualifications SPECIMEN ONLY

FOR OFFICIAL USE

Mark

SQ21/H/03

German Listening and Writing

Date — Not applicable
Duration — 1 hour

Fill in these boxes and read what is printed below.

Full name of centre

Town

Forename(s)

Surname

Number of seat

Date of birth
Day Month Year

Scottish candidate number

Total marks — 30

SECTION 1 — LISTENING — 20 marks

You will hear two items in German. **Before you hear each item, you will have one minute to study the questions.** You will hear each item twice, with an interval of one minute between playings. You will then have time to answer the questions before hearing the next item. Write your answers, in **English**, in the spaces provided.

SECTION 2 — WRITING — 10 marks

Write your answer, in **German**, in the space provided.

Attempt ALL questions. You may use a German dictionary.

Additional space for answers is provided at the end of this booklet. If you use this space you must clearly identify the question number you are attempting.

You are not allowed to leave the examination room until the end of the test.

Use **blue** or **black** ink.

Before leaving the examination room you must give this booklet to the Invigilator; if you do not, you may lose all the marks for this paper.

SECTION 1 — LISTENING — 20 marks

Attempt ALL questions

Item 1

You listen to a German radio report about the current situation of families in Germany.

(a) A recent survey has shown that more children are being born in Germany. What evidence is there of this? State any **one** thing. **1**

(b) German families with young children still experience problems. What are these problems? State any **two** things. **2**

(c) More and more German fathers are becoming house husbands. When is this the case? State any **two** examples. **2**

(d) The German government wants to improve the situation of parents with young children.

   (i) In what way will this help families? **1**

   (ii) In what way will this help children? State any **one** thing. **1**

(e) Consider the report as a whole. Overall, what does the report say about the situation for families with young children? Tick (✓) the correct statement. **1**

The report highlights some positive changes and some ongoing difficulties.	
The report is extremely critical of the lack of support.	
The report highlights a significant improvement.	

Item 2

Bianca, a German teenager, talks about her family.

(a) Bianca is no longer an only child. Why is this? Give any **one** reason. **1**

(b) Why was the situation not so easy for her at first? State any **three** things. **3**

(c) What strategy did her parents use to improve things? State **two** things. **2**

(d) Bianca talks about housework.

    (i) Why it necessary to help with the housework in her home? State **two** things. **2**

    (ii) How has her mother divided the tasks? State any **two** things. **2**

(e) Bianca concludes that she is happy. Why is this? State any **two** things. **2**

SECTION 2 — WRITING — 10 marks

Bianca hat eine kleine Familie. Wie ist das mit dir? Hast du eine große Familie? Wie kommst du mit deiner Familie aus? Denkst du, dass es wichtig ist Geschwister zu haben? Warum?

Schreibe 120–150 Wörter zu diesen Fragen.

ADDITIONAL SPACE FOR ANSWERS

ADDITIONAL SPACE FOR ANSWERS

National Qualifications
SPECIMEN ONLY

SQ21/H/13

German
Listening Transcript

Date — Not applicable
Duration — 1 hour

This paper must not be seen by any candidate.

The material overleaf is provided for use in an emergency only (eg the recording or equipment proving faulty) or where permission has been given in advance by SQA for the material to be read to candidates with additional support needs. The material must be read exactly as printed.

Transcript — Higher

> **Instructions to reader(s):**
>
> For each item, read the English **once**, then read the German **twice**, with an interval of 1 minute between the two readings. On completion of the second reading, pause for the length of time indicated in brackets after the item, to allow the candidates to write their answers.
>
> Where special arrangements have been agreed in advance to allow the reading of the material, those sections marked **(f)** should be read by a female speaker and those marked **(m)** by a male; those sections marked **(t)** should be read by the teacher.

(t) Item 1

You listen to a German radio report about the current situation of families in Germany.

You now have one minute to study the questions for Item 1.

(m/f) In einer aktuellen Umfrage wurde die Situation von Familien in Deutschland analysiert.

Die neusten Resultate in der Statistik zeigen, dass mehr Kinder geboren werden und dass Deutschland nicht mehr das Land der Einzelkinder ist: Fast fünfzig Prozent der Kinder und Jugendlichen haben einen Bruder oder eine Schwester. Jedes fünfte Kind hat sogar zwei Geschwister. Diese Statistiken sind sehr positiv, trotzdem haben Eltern mit kleinen Kindern einige Schwierigkeiten.

Junge Familien haben oft große Probleme, einen Platz in einem Kindergarten zu finden. Und deshalb muss in vielen Fällen ein Elternteil mit dem Kind zu Hause bleiben und kann nicht arbeiten gehen. Meistens ist es die Mutter – aber mehr und mehr Väter in Deutschland akzeptieren ihre neue Rolle als "Hausmann" und kümmern sich um die Kinder statt zur Arbeit zu gehen. Das ist besonders dann der Fall, wenn die Mutter einen Universitätsabschluss, oder eine andere professionelle Karriere hat und somit mehr Geld verdient.

Die deutsche Regierung will die Situation von Eltern mit kleinen Kindern verbessern. Diese Familien sollen finanzielle Hilfe bekommen und jedes Kind im Alter von drei Jahren soll einen Kindergartenplatz haben. Außerdem soll es in der Zukunft mehr Ganztagsschulen geben, sodass der Schultag länger ist und die Kinder nicht alleine zu Hause sind.

Deutschland hat bereits sehr viel Geld in die Familienpolitik investiert, aber noch viel mehr Geld ist nötig, damit diese Pläne Realität werden.

(2 minutes)

(t) **Item 2**

Bianca, a German teenager, talks about her family.

You now have one minute to study the questions for Item 2.

(m) Hallo Bianca, danke, dass du am Telefon bist. Hast du Geschwister oder bist du ein Einzelkind?

(f) Ja, hallo – naja, ich bin eigentlich ein Einzelkind, aber meine Mutter hat nochmal geheiratet und jetzt habe ich einen Stiefbruder. Er heißt Markus.

(m) Aha, also eine Patchworkfamilie . . . kommst du gut mit deinem Stiefbruder aus?

(f) Naja, am Anfang war das nicht so einfach. Ich bin 17 Jahre alt und Markus ist fünf Jahre jünger. Wir haben verschiedene Interessen und manchmal hat es mich total genervt, dass er nur über Tennis gesprochen hat. Ich interessiere mich nicht für Sport und gehe lieber mit meinen Freunden ins Kino oder in ein Popkonzert.

(m) Und wie ist die Situation jetzt?

(f) Hmmm . . . es funktioniert ganz gut, denke ich. Unsere Eltern haben eine Strategie, damit wir uns besser kennen lernen: Ein Wochenende gehen wir alle in den Tennisklub um ein Spiel zu sehen und am anderen Wochenende gehen wir alle ins Kino. Ich kann jetzt besser verstehen, warum Markus ein Tennisfan ist – ein Spiel kann sehr spannend sein.

(m) Und geht Markus jetzt auch gern ins Kino?

(f) Naja, nein, nicht wirklich. Er akzeptiert es, wenn wir einen neuen Film sehen wollen, aber Markus ist super sportlich und fit – er ist lieber an der frischen Luft als im Kino.

(m) Gibt es etwas, was ihr beide gemeinsam macht?

(f) Ja, klar! Die Hausarbeit. Wir beide helfen jeden Tag im Haushalt, weil beide Eltern arbeiten und Markus' Vater oft Spätschicht hat – er ist Polizist.

(m) Oh je, und wie klappt das?

(f) Meine Mutter ist total organisiert und hat einen Haushaltsplan gemacht. Jeder in der Familie hat eine Aufgabe. Markus muss staubsaugen und ich muss den Geschirrspüler und die Waschmaschine beladen und entladen. Außerdem müssen wir gemeinsam mit dem Hund Gassi gehen und jeder muss sein Zimmer aufräumen.

(m) Was findest du besser – Einzelkind sein oder Geschwister haben?

(f) Naja, ich denke, dass es schon toll ist, wenn man eine große Familie und Geschwister hat. Es ist immer jemand da, wenn man ein Problem hat und mit jemandem darüber reden möchte. Ja, doch, ich bin sehr froh, dass ich meinen Stiefbruder habe!

(m) Danke, Bianca, hast du einen Musikwunsch?

(f) Oh, ja, prima . . . Markus und ich hören sehr gern Neue Deutsche Welle. Ein Lied in dem Stil wäre cool.

(2 minutes)

(t) **End of test.**

Now look over your answers.

[END OF SPECIMEN TRANSCRIPT]

HIGHER FOR CfE

Model Paper 1

Whilst this Model Practice Paper has been specially commissioned by Hodder Gibson for use as practice for the Higher (for Curriculum for Excellence) exams, the key reference document remains the SQA Specimen Paper 2014.

National Qualifications
MODEL PAPER 1

German Reading

Duration — 1 hour and 40 minutes

Total marks — 30

Attempt ALL questions.

Write your answers clearly, in **English**, in the Reading Answer Booklet provided. In the answer booklet you must clearly identify the question number you are attempting.

You may use a German dictionary.

Use **blue** or **black** ink.

There is a separate question and answer booklet for Directed Writing. You must complete your answer for Directed Writing in the question and answer booklet for Directed Writing.

Before leaving the examination room you must give your Reading answer booklet and your Directed Writing answer booklet to the Invigilator; if you do not, you may lose all the marks for this paper.

Total marks — 30

Read the whole article carefully and then answer, in English, ALL the questions that follow.

The article discusses the role of minority languages in the European Union.

Haben Minderheitensprachen eine Zukunft?

Sprache bedeutet viel mehr als nur Kommunikation — sie ist eine Grundlage der Kultur. Innerhalb der Europäischen Union sprechen etwa 46 Millionen Bürger mit großem Stolz eine Minderheitssprache.

Doch viele europäische Minderheitensprachen sind bereits lautlos untergegangen: Erst
5 wurden sie von immer weniger Menschen gesprochen. Dann wurden sie auch an Schulen nicht mehr unterrichtet. Dabei gehört gerade die Sprache zur Identität eines Volkes: Sie ist verbunden mit besonderem Brauchtum, einer langen Geschichte und einer ganz eigenen Kultur.

In vielen europäischen Ländern werden diese Regionalsprachen von der nationalen
10 Regierung finanziell gefördert — zum Beispiel Gälisch in Schottland oder Katalanisch in Spanien. Sie werden als Unterrichtssprache in manchen Schulen verwendet und sind auf zweisprachigen Straßenschildern und in Stadtzentren zu sehen.

Auch im Norden von Deutschland existiert eine Minderheitensprache: Plattdeutsch. Allerdings ist diese vom Aussterben bedroht, obwohl die Regierungen von Schleswig-Holstein
15 und Mecklenburg-Vorpommern alles tun, um diese Sprache zu schützen. Aber ist das wirklich erfolgreich?

Kurz vor dem Mittagessen ist im Kindergarten, in der norddeutschen Stadt Aurich, Zeit für die Geschichte „Dicker, fetter Pfannkuchen". Etwa 15 Kinder sitzen im Stuhlkreis um Kindergärtnerin Maria Schmidt herum, die ihnen die Geschichte vorliest und sie immer
20 wieder zum Weitererzählen ermuntert — all das auf Plattdeutsch. Denn dieser Kindergarten ist seit mehr als zehn Jahren zweisprachig.

Maria Schmidt ist eine von den Kindergärtnerinnen, die immer Plattdeutsch mit den Kindern sprechen, andere dagegen sprechen immer Hochdeutsch — egal, ob beim Frühstück, beim Händewaschen oder Basteln. Manchmal holt Maria Schmidt auch Karten mit aufgemalten
25 Symbolen heraus und fragt die Kinder, wie die jeweiligen Begriffe — beispielsweise Stuhl, Schrank oder Schere - auf Plattdeutsch heißen.

„Wir merken, dass immer weniger Kinder schon mit Plattdeutsch zu uns kommen", sagt Schmidt, die in Norddeutschland geboren ist. „Aber sie gewöhnen sich schnell daran und wenn sie mal etwas nicht verstehen, dann übersetzt ein anderes Kind oder wir erklären mit
30 Gestik oder Mimik, was wir meinen."

Eine Umfrage unter Jugendlichen in Norddeutschland hat vor kurzem gezeigt, dass zwar 50 Prozent von ihnen noch Plattdeutsch verstehen, aber nur 20 Prozent es auch sprechen — das ist zu wenig um die Sprache zu bewahren. Deshalb wird in über 60 Kindergärten in der Region seit einigen Jahren auch Plattdeutsch gesprochen.

35 Manche Experten befürchten, dass es zu spät ist und Plattdeutsch langsam ausstirbt. Vor allem hat diese Sprache ein Imageproblem: Sie gilt bei vielen jüngeren Menschen in der Region als Sprache der Landbevölkerung. „Es gibt hier Menschen, die negative Ideen gegenüber Plattdeutsch haben und sagen: ‚Wir wollen und brauchen die Sprache nicht mehr, das ist Geschichte, lasst uns damit in Ruhe'", sagt Susanne Fischer, Bildungsforscherin
40 an der Universität Osnabrück. Außerdem beklagt sie, dass Eltern zu Unrecht denken, dass Kinder, die mit Plattdeutsch aufwachsen, später kein Verständnis für Hochdeutsch haben.

Fischer und ihre Mitarbeiter wollen dagegen ankämpfen — unter anderem mit dem Projekt der dreisprachigen Grundschule. Deutsch und Plattdeutsch sind von Anfang an Unterrichtssprachen, in der dritten Klasse kommt Englisch noch hinzu. „Wir machen die
45 Erfahrung, dass Kinder, die mit Plattdeutsch aufwachsen, sich auch des Hochdeutschen viel bewusster sind", sagt sie. Fischer selbst ist keine gebürtige Norddeutsche und hat erst später Plattdeutsch gelernt. „Aber ich lerne gern von den Einheimischen", sagt sie.

Zehn Kilometer entfernt von Aurich arbeitet Pastor Andreas Müller im Ort Holtrop — auch er ist kein Platt-Muttersprachler. Vor 15 Jahren zog er aus Ostdeutschland in den äußersten
50 Nordwesten Deutschlands und merkte schnell: Ein „Moin, Moin" zur Begrüßung reicht hier nicht. Denn für viele seiner Gemeindemitglieder, vor allem für die Älteren, ist Plattdeutsch Alltags- und Muttersprache.

<u>Deswegen meldete sich Andreas für Sprachkurse an der örtlichen Volkshochschule an und suchte im Dorf nach geduldigen Privatlehrern. Heute hält er manchmal auch Gottesdienst
55 auf Plattdeutsch — und sagt, dass er die Sprache sehr zu schätzen gelernt hat:</u> „Es ist eine bilderreiche und einfache Sprache, die sehr direkt ist — damit kommt man den Menschen hier schnell sehr nah."

MARKS

Questions

Re-read lines 1–12

1. According to the text, languages are about much more than communication.

   (a) What is the current situation of minority languages in the European Union? State **two** things. — 2

   (b) What are the reasons for this situation? State **two** things. — 2

2. Languages are part of the identity of people. Why is this? Give any **two** details. — 2

3. Many EU countries support minority languages. In what way do they support them? Give any **two** details. — 2

Re-read lines 13–21

4. A minority language, Low German, is spoken in the north of Germany. What is the current status of the language? State **two** things. — 2

5. In a nursery school in Aurich, stories are told in Low German.

   (a) What happens during story-time in class? Give any **two** details. — 2

   (b) Why is this particular nursery school different from other nursery schools? State **one** thing. — 1

MARKS

Re-read lines 22–30

6. Maria Schmidt always speaks Low German with her pupils.

    (a) On which three occasions does she speak Low German? Give **three** details. 1

    (b) In what other way does she support pupils when she speaks Low German? State any **one** thing. 1

7. She continues by telling us that fewer and fewer pupils arrive to the nursery school being able to speak Low German. What does she say about these pupils? Give any **one** detail. 1

Re-read lines 31–41

8. Many experts are worried that it is too late to save Low German. Why is this? State any **one** thing. 1

9. According to Susanne Fischer, what is the advantage of children who grow up with Low German? State **one** thing. 1

10. Now consider the article as a whole. Is the author optimistic about the future of minority languages in the EU? Give reasons for your answer with reference to the text. 2

11. Translate into English:

    "Deswegen meldete .... gelernt hat." (*lines 53–55*) 10

[END OF MODEL QUESTION PAPER]

Page four

FOR OFFICIAL USE

National Qualifications
MODEL PAPER 1

Mark

German
Directed Writing

Duration — 1 hour and 40 minutes

Fill in these boxes and read what is printed below.

Full name of centre

Town

Forename(s)

Surname

Number of seat

Date of birth
Day Month Year

Scottish candidate number

Total marks — 10

Choose ONE scenario on *Page two* and write your answer clearly, in **German**, in the space provided in this booklet. You must clearly identify the scenario number you are attempting.

You may use a German dictionary.

Additional space for answers is provided at the end of this booklet.

Use **blue** or **black** ink.

There is a separate answer booklet for Reading. You must complete your answers for Reading in the answer booklet for Reading.

Before leaving the examination room you must give this Directed Writing question and answer booklet and your Reading answer booklet to the Invigilator; if you do not, you may lose all the marks for this paper.

Total marks — 10

Choose **one** of the following two scenarios.

SCENARIO 1: Learning

> During the Easter holidays, you went on a school exchange to Berlin in Germany.
>
> On your return, you write an article **in German** for the Modern Languages section of your school's/college's website.

You must include the following information and **you should try to add** other relevant details:

- how you travelled **and** what the school was like
- what you did during the school day
- what you did in your free time
- how you plan to stay in contact with your exchange partner in the future

You should write approximately 120–150 words.

OR

SCENARIO 2: Employability

> Last year, you spent the summer working in a hotel in Germany to gain some work experience.
>
> On your return, your teacher asks you to write **in German** about the experience.

You must include the following information and **you should try to add** other relevant details:

- where exactly the hotel was **and** what the accommodation was like
- what your duties were
- how you got on with your colleagues
- whether you would recommend working abroad to others

You should write approximately 120–150 words.

Scenario number

ANSWER SPACE (continued)

ANSWER SPACE (continued)

ANSWER SPACE (continued)

[END OF MODEL QUESTION PAPER]

ADDITIONAL SPACE FOR ANSWERS

ADDITIONAL SPACE FOR ANSWERS

FOR OFFICIAL USE

National Qualifications
MODEL PAPER 1

Mark

German
Listening and Writing

Duration — 1 hour

Fill in these boxes and read what is printed below.

Full name of centre

Town

Forename(s)

Surname

Number of seat

Date of birth
Day Month Year

Scottish candidate number

Total marks — 30

SECTION 1 — LISTENING — 20 marks

You will hear two items in German. **Before you hear each item, you will have one minute to study the questions.** You will hear each item twice, with an interval of one minute between playings. You will then have time to answer the questions before hearing the next item. Write your answers, in **English**, in the spaces provided.

SECTION 2 — WRITING — 10 marks

Write your answer, in **German**, in the space provided.

Attempt ALL questions. You may use a German dictionary.

Additional space for answers is provided at the end of this booklet. If you use this space you must clearly identify the question number you are attempting.

You are not allowed to leave the examination room until the end of the test.

Use **blue** or **black** ink.

Before leaving the examination room you must give this booklet to the Invigilator; if you do not, you may lose all the marks for this paper.

SECTION 1 — LISTENING — 20 marks

Attempt ALL questions

Item 1

You listen to a German radio report about tourists visiting Germany.

(a) According to the latest statistics, the number of foreign visitors has increased. What evidence is there of this? State any **one** thing. **1**

(b) According to the passage, what are the main reasons for tourists to visit Germany? State any **two** things. **2**

(c) According to the report, what are the advantages of Germany as a tourist destination? State **two** things. **2**

(d) Berlin is a great tourist attraction. Why is this? State any **one** thing. **1**

(e) Many students also come to Germany to study. Why is this? State any **one** thing. **1**

(f) Consider the report as a whole. Overall, what does the report say about tourism in Germany? Tick (✓) the correct statement. **1**

The report is an advertisement to encourage tourists to come to Germany.	
The report highlights why many tourists and students come to Germany.	
The report highlights the future potential of Germany's tourist sector.	

Item 2

Sarah, a German exchange student, speaks to Paul on his return from his gap year in Germany.

(a) Paul has just spent a year in Germany.

    (i) When did he arrive home? **1**

    (ii) In which part of Germany did he live? **1**

(b) During his time he stayed with a host family. What does he say about his arrival? State any **one** thing. **1**

(c) What does he say about his host brother? State any **two** things. **2**

(d) He talks about some aspects of German life.

    (i) What does he say about his time at school? State any **one** thing. **1**

    (ii) What does he say about the free time of German pupils? State **one** thing. **1**

(e) What did he enjoy most about his time in Germany? State any **two** things. **2**

(f) He says that he will miss his experience in Germany.

    (i) In what ways has he benefited from his time there? State any **two** things. **2**

    (ii) What are his plans for the future? State any **one** thing. **1**

SECTION 2 — WRITING — 10 marks

Paul hat über sein Brückenjahr in Deutschland gesprochen. Wie ist das mit dir? Hast du Fremdsprachenkenntnisse? Möchtest du ein Jahr in einem anderen Land leben? Wohin würdest du fahren?

Schreibe 120–150 Wörter zu diesen Fragen.

ADDITIONAL SPACE FOR ANSWERS

ADDITIONAL SPACE FOR ANSWERS

National Qualifications
MODEL PAPER 1

German
Listening Transcript

Duration — 1 hour

This paper must not be seen by any candidate.

The material overleaf is provided for use in an emergency only (eg the recording or equipment proving faulty) or where permission has been given in advance by SQA for the material to be read to candidates with additional support needs. The material must be read exactly as printed.

Transcript — Higher

Instructions to reader(s):

For each item, read the English **once**, then read the German **twice**, with an interval of 1 minute between the two readings. On completion of the second reading, pause for the length of time indicated in brackets after the item, to allow the candidates to write their answers.

Where special arrangements have been agreed in advance to allow the reading of the material, those sections marked **(f)** should be read by a female speaker and those marked **(m)** by a male; those sections marked **(t)** should be read by the teacher.

(t) Item 1

You listen to a report about Germany as a tourist destination.

You now have one minute to study the questions for Item 1.

(m/f) Tourismusexperten haben vor kurzem über Deutschland als Reiseziel diskutiert.

Immer mehr ausländische Gäste wählen Deutschland als Reiseziel, wie eine aktuelle Statistik zeigt: In der ersten Hälfte des Jahres kamen 17 Millionen Gäste aus dem Ausland nach Deutschland. Das waren 7% mehr als im Vorjahr.

Durch seine lange Geschichte und reiche Kultur bietet Deutschland viele interessante Sehenswürdigkeiten. Der Kölner Dom etwa zählt zu den weltweit beliebtesten Kulturdenkmälern, und auch verschiedene Naturlandschaften, wie die Alpen, ziehen viele Urlauber an.

Es ist kein Wunder, dass Deutschland so beliebt ist — das Land hat viel zu bieten. Deutschland ist preiswerter als andere europäische Reiseziele und Reisende fühlen sich hier sicher. Die erstklassigen Verkehrsverbindungen erlauben Besuchern andere Städte im Land zu entdecken.

Eine ganz besondere Touristenattraktion ist die Bundeshauptstadt Berlin. Als Sitz der Regierung und Stadt voller Geschichte ist Berlin zum Brennpunkt geworden. Die multikulturelle Stadt hat auch viele Kunstgalerien, Museen und man kann immer noch die Reste der Berliner Mauer sehen.

Viele ausländische Studenten wollen in Deutschland studieren und manche verbringen hier sogar ein Auslandsemester, um die Deutschen näher kennen zu lernen. Mit den USA und Großbritannien ist die Bundesrepublik eins der beliebtesten Ziele für Studienplätze. Viele Studenten kommen nach Deutschland, um ihre Sprachkenntnisse zu verbessern, die akademischen Institute und die Qualifikationen sind überall anerkannt.

(2 minutes)

(t) **Item 2**

Sarah, a German exchange student, speaks to Paul on his return from a gap-year in Germany.

You now have one minute to study the questions for Item 2.

(f) **Hallo Paul! Schon lange nicht mehr gesehen. Seit wann bist du wieder da? Du warst letztes Jahr in Deutschland, oder?**

(m) Ja, hallo — ich bin erst vorgestern angekommen. Ich habe zehn Monate in einem kleinen Dorf im Südwesten verbracht, wo ich bei einer Gastfamilie gewohnt habe.

(f) **Ja stimmt, und wie war das so bei einer deutschen Gastfamilie zu wohnen?**

(m) Weißt du, es war echt toll, aber am Anfang war es doch schwierig, da ich ein bisschen Heimweh hatte und ich nicht alles verstanden habe. Sie haben viel zu schnell gesprochen und ich musste mich ein bisschen dran gewöhnen, weil sie einen sehr starken Akzent hatten. Aber die Hauptsache war, dass sie mit mir geduldig waren.

(f) **Und bist du mit ihnen gut ausgekommen?**

(m) Ja schon, im Großen und Ganzen haben wir uns prima verstanden. Mein Gastbruder war so alt wie ich und ich habe sein Zimmer mit ihm geteilt. Wir hatten viele gemeinsame Interessen und wir waren auch in derselben Klasse in der Schule, so konnten wir unsere Hausaufgaben zusammen machen.

(f) **Und wie fandest du die Schule?**

(m) Es hat mir wirklich Spaß gemacht in Deutschland in die Schule zu gehen. Meine Mitschüler haben sich für mich interessiert und ich habe viel von Schottland erzählt, besonders natürlich im Englischunterricht. Da war ich meist Mittelpunkt der Klasse

(f) **Und wie war es mit der Freizeit?**

(m) Deutsche Schüler haben viel Freizeit und viele Hobbys. Die Schule ist schon früh am Nachmittag zu Ende — so gegen zwei oder drei Uhr. Viele Schüler sind in Vereinen, weil es in der Schule wenig Freizeitangebote gibt. Ich war im Handballverein. Das war toll, da ich viele neue Freunde getroffen habe.

(f) **Was hat dir am besten gefallen?**

(m) In Schottland wäre es unvorstellbar, dass alle Geschäfte sonntags geschlossen sind. Man konnte also viel Zeit mit der Familie verbringen — wir sind oft in den Bergen gewandert — bis zu einem See, wo man baden und windsurfen konnte. Die Aussicht war atemberaubend und die Luft war sehr sauber.

(f) **Wird dir diese Erfahrung fehlen?**

(m) Ja, es war echt Spitze. Ich habe von meiner Zeit in Deutschland profitiert. Mein Deutsch hat sich verbessert und ich habe einen Einblick in den deutschen Alltag bekommen. Ich würde sagen, dass ich noch mehr Selbstvertrauen habe und ich habe auch Lust, andere Länder zu besuchen. Ich habe viele neue Freunde kennen gelernt und wir werden in Kontakt bleiben. Ich habe vor, Fremdsprachen an der Uni zu studieren, so dass ich noch ein Jahr im Ausland verbringen kann. Ich würde jedem empfehlen einen Aufenthalt in Deutschland zu verbringen.

Item 2 (continued)

(f)   Super, Paul. Ich freue mich, dass es dir in Deutschland gefallen hat.   Und dein Deutsch ist echt toll.

(2 minutes)

(t)   End of test.

Now look over your answers.

[END OF MODEL TRANSCRIPT]

HIGHER FOR CfE

Model Paper 2

Whilst this Model Practice Paper has been specially commissioned by Hodder Gibson for use as practice for the Higher (for Curriculum for Excellence) exams, the key reference document remains the SQA Specimen Paper 2014.

National
Qualifications
MODEL PAPER 2

German Reading

Duration — 1 hour and 40 minutes

Total marks — 30

Attempt ALL questions.

Write your answers clearly, in **English**, in the Reading Answer Booklet provided. In the answer booklet you must clearly identify the question number you are attempting.

You may use a German dictionary.

Use **blue** or **black** ink.

There is a separate question and answer booklet for Directed Writing. You must complete your answer for Directed Writing in the question and answer booklet for Directed Writing.

Before leaving the examination room you must give your Reading answer booklet and your Directed Writing answer booklet to the Invigilator; if you do not, you may lose all the marks for this paper.

Total marks — 30

Read the whole article carefully and then answer, in English, ALL the questions that follow.

The article discusses different attitudes to bad school reports.

Zeugnisstress — muss das sein?

In Englisch eine Sechs, in Latein auch ... und wenn der Rest der Zeugnisnoten auch nicht besonders toll ist, drohen vielen Schülerinnen und Schülern zu Hause Ärger und ganz viel Druck. Doch diese Reaktion der Eltern bringt gar nichts, im Gegenteil, da sind sich die Experten sicher.

5 Paul, Schüler am Gymnasium, hat gestern ein schlechtes Zeugnis bekommen. Seine Eltern haben mit Enttäuschung und Vorwürfen reagiert und als Konsequenz das Fußballspielen verboten. Der Schulpsychologe Lars Hoffmann warnt Eltern vor solchen Maßnahmen, denn es sind ja oft die Bereiche, in denen der Jugendliche außerhalb der Schule noch Erfolgserlebnisse hat. „Wenn man ihm diese verbietet, hat er nichts mehr, worin er gut ist,
10 und das ist alles andere als motivierend. Und Motivation ist der Schlüssel zum Erfolg!"

Die Art und Weise, wie man diese Situation behandelt, ist umstritten. Schülerberaterin Anna Vogt erzählt von ihren Erfahrung mit Eltern, die mit schlechten Noten konfrontiert wurden: „Die Reaktion der Eltern ist unterschiedlich. Manche sind wütend und geben den Lehrern die Schuld. Andere wollen wissen, wie sie dabei helfen können. Und dann gibt es
15 auch Eltern, denen das alles nicht so wichtig erscheint." Frau Vogt ist der Meinung, dass Druck von den Eltern Angst erzeugt und Angst das Gehirn blockiert. Um bessere Fortschritte zu machen, sollten Eltern auf die Zukunft konzentrieren und gemeinsam überlegen, was man besser machen kann. Eltern sollten ihr Kind ganz konkret fragen: Wie können wir dir dabei helfen?

20 Für viele Bildungsexperten zeigen Zeugnisse nur den aktuellen Stand des Schülers an und nicht, wie er sich entwickelt hat, ob er sich angestrengt und bemüht hat. Die Qualität der Beziehung zwischen Lehrer und Schüler und das Klassenklima sind wichtig für den Erfolg. Man sollte kurzfristig planen und kleine Schritte machen. Es bringt nichts, ein ganzes Schuljahr im Voraus zu planen, welche Noten der Schüler auf dem nächsten Zeugnis haben
25 soll. Der Zeitraum ist viel zu lang und nicht angemessen. Eltern, die sich ernsthaft für ihr Kind und seinen Lernerfolg interessieren, sollten es ermutigen, anspornen und realistische Ziele setzen, die erreichbar sind.

„Nicht alle Fächer sind in den Augen der Eltern wertvoll," meint Englischlehrer Kai Jones. „Sie
30 erfahren auch nicht, ob sich ihr Kind Mühe gegeben hat, Zeit investiert, Vokabeln gelernt und Hausaufgaben gemacht hat. Es gibt Kinder, die sind nicht besonders sprachbegabt und bekommen in Englisch eine Drei oder Vier auf dem Zeugnis, und die Eltern sollen diese Leistung auch loben. Man soll Schüler nicht vergleichen."

Laut einer Studie bekommen die Hälfte der befragten Schüler Geschenke als Lob bei guten Zeugnissen. Dies kann motivierend sein, aber wenn man seinem Kind eine Belohnung
35 versprechen will, dann sollte es eine soziale und keine materielle Belohnung sein. Es ist zwar einfacher, einen materiellen Wunsch zu erfüllen, effektiver ist aber beispielsweise zusammen ins Kino zu gehen, gemeinsam einen Ausflug zu machen oder wenn die Eltern mit dem Kind am Wochenende Zelten geht.

Es sind nicht nur die Eltern, die daran denken sollen. Schüler haben eine gewisse
40 Verantwortung für Zeugnisse und ihre Noten zu tragen. Sie müssen aktiv Hilfe suchen und müssen Lernstrategien entwickeln. Es ist wichtig, dass Schüler nicht gleich anfangen zu lernen, wenn sie aus der Schule kommen. Körper und Geist brauchen eine Erholungspause, um frische Energie zu tanken — joggen, Musik hören oder ein Buch lesen helfen dabei.

Genau wie der Körper beim Sport braucht auch der Kopf ein bisschen Zeit, um
45 warmzulaufen. Deswegen soll man deswegen immer mit den einfachen Aufgaben beginnen und erst mit den schweren Sachen später anfangen.

Auch Kai Jones gibt den Schülern ein paar Lerntipps: „Versuche, deinen eigenen Lernrhythmus zu finden. Lerne jeden Tag zur gleichen Zeit — so merkst du dir den Stoff leichter und die Aufgaben sammeln sich nicht zu einem Berg an, den du irgendwann nicht
50 mehr bewältigen kannst. Wenn du jeden Tag dein Ziel erledigst, werden sich nicht nur deine Noten verbessern, sondern auch deine Laune."

Alle unsere Experten sind grundsätzlich der Meinung: Schulprobleme löst man in der Schulzeit! Und Ferien sind Ferien!

Questions

MARKS

Re-read lines 1–10

1. According to the text, many pupils receive bad grades on their report cards. What is the reaction at home? State **two** things. — **2**

2. Paul is one of these pupils who recently received a bad report.

   (a) In what way did his parents react? Give any **two** details. — **2**

   (b) Lars Hoffman, the school psychologist, does not approve. Why is this? Give **three** details. — **3**

Re-read lines 11–27

3. According to pupil councillor, Anna Vogt, in what way do parents generally respond to bad grades? State any **two** things. — **2**

4. According to the text, what should parents do to help pupils' progress? Give any **three** details. — **3**

5. According to a study, half of pupils receive a present for a good report card.

   (a) What advice is there about the type of reward that parents should give? State **one** thing. — **1**

   (b) What examples of presents does the text mention? Give any **two** details. — **2**

Re-read lines 39–51

6. According to the text, what can pupils do to improve their grades? State any **two** things. — **2**

7. What is the experts' overall opinion on school problems? State **one** thing. — **1**

	MARKS
8. Now consider the article as a whole. Does the writer believe that school reports are a good or a bad thing? Give reasons for your answer with reference to the text.	2
9. Translate into English: "Nicht alle Fächer .... gemacht hat." (*lines 28–30*)	10

[END OF MODEL QUESTION PAPER]

H

FOR OFFICIAL USE

National
Qualifications
MODEL PAPER 2

Mark

German
Directed Writing

Duration — 1 hour and 40 minutes

Fill in these boxes and read what is printed below.

Full name of centre

Town

Forename(s)

Surname

Number of seat

Date of birth
Day   Month   Year

Scottish candidate number

Total marks — 10

Choose ONE scenario on *Page two* and write your answer clearly, in **German**, in the space provided in this booklet. You must clearly identify the scenario number you are attempting.

You may use a German dictionary.

Additional space for answers is provided at the end of this booklet.

Use **blue** or **black** ink.

There is a separate answer booklet for Reading. You must complete your answers for Reading in the answer booklet for Reading.

Before leaving the examination room you must give this Directed Writing question and answer booklet and your Reading answer booklet to the Invigilator; if you do not, you may lose all the marks for this paper.

Total marks — 10

Choose **one** of the following two scenarios.

SCENARIO 1: Employability

> Last week, you were invited to an interview in Austria for a summer job at a holiday camp.
>
> On your return, your teacher asks you to write **in German** about your experience.

You must include the following information and **you should try to add** other relevant details:

- how you travelled **and** what the accommodation was like
- how you prepared for the job interview
- what you thought about the interview
- what duties your job will include

You should write approximately 120–150 words.

OR

SCENARIO 2: Culture

> Last February, you travelled to Cologne with a group of friends to celebrate *Karneval*.
>
> On your return, your teacher asks you to write **in German** about your experience.

You must include the following information and **you should try to add** other relevant details:

- how you travelled **and** what the journey was like
- what you did during your stay
- what you liked/dislike most about the experience
- whether you would return to Germany

You should write approximately 120–150 words.

Scenario number

ANSWER SPACE (continued)

ANSWER SPACE (continued)

[END OF MODEL QUESTION PAPER]

ADDITIONAL SPACE FOR ANSWERS

ADDITIONAL SPACE FOR ANSWERS

FOR OFFICIAL USE

National Qualifications
MODEL PAPER 2

Mark

German
Listening and Writing

Duration — 1 hour

Fill in these boxes and read what is printed below.

Full name of centre

Town

Forename(s)

Surname

Number of seat

Date of birth
Day   Month   Year

Scottish candidate number

Total marks — 30

SECTION 1 — LISTENING — 20 marks

You will hear two items in German. **Before you hear each item, you will have one minute to study the questions.** You will hear each item twice, with an interval of one minute between playings. You will then have time to answer the questions before hearing the next item. Write your answers, in **English**, in the spaces provided.

SECTION 2 — WRITING — 10 marks

Write your answer, in **German**, in the space provided.

Attempt ALL questions. You may use a German dictionary.

Additional space for answers is provided at the end of this booklet. If you use this space you must clearly identify the question number you are attempting.

You are not allowed to leave the examination room until the end of the test.

Use **blue** or **black** ink.

Before leaving the examination room you must give this booklet to the Invigilator; if you do not, you may lose all the marks for this paper.

SECTION 1 — LISTENING — 20 marks

Attempt ALL questions

Item 1

You listen to a German radio report about young people and new technology in Germany.

(a) A recent study has shown that more and more young people are using the internet. What evidence is there of this? State any **one** thing. **1**

(b) There are still a number of problems associated with new technology. What are these problems? Give any **two** details. **2**

(c) There are also advantages of new technology. What are these advantages? State **two** things. **2**

(d) Many schools in Bavaria are considering allowing pupils to use their own devices in class.

  (i) In what way will this help young people? State any **one** thing. **1**

  (ii) Critics have also voiced their concerns. What do they claim may happen? State any **one** thing. **1**

(e) Consider the report as a whole. Overall, what does the report say about young people's relationship with new technology? Tick (✓) the correct statement. **1**

The report is extremely critical of new technology.	
The report highlights some positive and negative impacts of new technology.	
The report highlights that young people are sensible with new technology.	

Item 2

Peter talks to Silke about her new smartphone.

(a) Silke has just got a new smartphone. When **and** why did she get it? **1**

(b) Silke thinks she needs a smartphone. Why is this? State any **two** things. **2**

(c) What does she do to pay for the phone bill? State any **two** things. **2**

(d) In what way can her mobile phone help with her homework? State **two** things. **2**

(e) Silke talks about mobile phones at her school. What does she say? State any **two** things. **2**

(f) Silke talks about what happened to her friend's phone. What does she say? Give any **two** details. **2**

(g) What is she doing at the weekend? State any **one** thing. **1**

SECTION 2 — WRITING — 10 marks

Silke ist sehr zufrieden mit ihrem neuen Smartphone. Wie ist das mit dir? Hast du auch ein Handy? Surfst du oft im Internet? Was sind die Vor- und Nachteile der neuen Medien?

Schreibe 120–150 Wörter zu diesen Fragen.

ADDITIONAL SPACE FOR ANSWERS

ADDITIONAL SPACE FOR ANSWERS

National Qualifications
MODEL PAPER 2

German
Listening Transcript

Duration — 1 hour

This paper must not be seen by any candidate.

The material overleaf is provided for use in an emergency only (eg the recording or equipment proving faulty) or where permission has been given in advance by SQA for the material to be read to candidates with additional support needs. The material must be read exactly as printed.

Transcript — Higher

> **Instructions to reader(s):**
>
> For each item, read the English **once**, then read the German **twice**, with an interval of 1 minute between the two readings. On completion of the second reading, pause for the length of time indicated in brackets after the item, to allow the candidates to write their answers.
>
> Where special arrangements have been agreed in advance to allow the reading of the material, those sections marked **(f)** should be read by a female speaker and those marked **(m)** by a male; those sections marked **(t)** should be read by the teacher.

(t) **Item 1**

You listen to a German radio report about young people and new technology in Germany.

You now have one minute to study the questions for Item 1.

(m/f) In einer aktuellen Umfrage wurde die Situation der neuen Medien in Deutschland analysiert.

Laut den Ergebnissen einer neuen Studie verbringen Jugendliche immer mehr Zeit im Internet: Fast neunzig Prozent der Kinder und Jugendlichen haben heutzutage ein Handy und Internetzugang. Drei Viertel der Befragten haben sogar ein Smartphone.

Obwohl die Verwendung der neuen Technologien zwar als positiv betrachtet wird, tauchen auch neue Probleme auf. Erstens stehen Eltern unter Druck, das neuste Gerät für ihre Kinder zu kaufen. In vielen Fällen können sich die Familien wegen der finanziellen Kosten ein neues Smartphone oder Tablet nicht leisten. Zweitens machen sich viele Eltern, Politiker und Gesundheitsexperten Sorgen darum, dass Jugendliche sich nicht mehr konzentrieren können und weniger Zeit mit Freunden verbringen.

Natürlich bringen die neuen Technologien auch viele Vorteile. Man kann immer mit Familie und Freunden in Kontakt bleiben und das Internet hilft Schülern dabei, Information schnell zu finden. Deswegen diskutieren nun viele Schulen in Bayern, ob Schüler ihre eigenen Geräte im Klassenzimmer benutzen dürfen. Viele meinen, dass es dabei helfen würde, Jugendliche besser auf die Zukunft vorzubereiten und Schüler mit verschiedenen Lernstilen unterstützen könnte. Kritiker befürchten, dass dies eine negative Wirkung auf die sozialen Fähigkeiten der Schüler haben wird und dass Lehrer während des Unterrichts von Schülern gefilmt werden könnten.

Das größte Problem aber besteht darin, dass manche Schulen technisch nicht sehr gut ausgerüstet sind. Deswegen müsste die Regierung viel Geld investieren, das für andere Sachen ausgegeben werden kann.

(2 minutes)

(t) **Item 2**

Peter talks to Silke about her new smartphone.

You now have one minute to study the questions for Item 2.

(m) Hallo Silke, was hast du denn da?

(f) Ja, hallo Onkel Peter — magst du mein neues Smartphone, das ich letzte Woche zum Geburtstag bekommen habe? Meine Eltern haben's mir geschenkt.

(m) Ah ja, was für ein tolles Geschenk — sieht sehr schick aus! Aber brauchst so ein teures Ding?

(f) Ja, klar! Alle meine Freunde haben auch solche Handys, so können wir alle per SMS in Kontakt bleiben — es ist wirklich sehr praktisch! Man kann auch Musik herunterladen, online fernsehen und auf dem Handy spielen. Schau mal.

(m) Und wer bezahlt das alles?

(f) Hallo… ich muss die Handyrechnung selber zahlen! Ich arbeite Teilzeit am Wochenende im Supermarkt und ich muss auch im Haushalt helfen, das heißt, ich staubsauge jeden Tag und muss mit dem Hund im Park spazieren gehen. Außerdem kümmere ich mich um meinen Bruder, wenn meine Eltern einkaufen gehen oder ins Kino wollen — dafür bekomme ich mein Taschengeld. Siehst du, ich kann Verantwortung tragen.

(m) Ja und jetzt verbringst du die ganze Zeit auf Facebook und was ist mit deinen Hausaufgaben?

(f) Naja, nein, nicht wirklich. Das Handy hat auch Internetzugang, somit kann es mir bei den Hausaufgaben helfen, besonders wenn Vati den Computer benutzt. Dadurch kann ich viel Zeit sparen und meine Antworten mit meinen Freunden prüfen, wenn ich etwas nicht verstehe! Schau mal, es hat auch ein Wörterbuch für den Englischunterricht drin — man kann die Wörter viel schneller nachschlagen. Ich kann auch hören, wie man die neuen Vokabeln richtig ausspricht!

(m) Ach so, darfst du's in der Schule benutzen?

(f) Naja, es kommt drauf an. Manche Lehrer erlauben es uns, manche nicht. Auf jeden Fall dürfen wir es während der Pause benutzen, aber wir kriegen Ärger wenn es in der Klasse klingelt. Manche Schüler spielen mit dem Handy und hören gar nicht zu — wenn der Lehrer sie erwischt, dann wird das Handy weggenommen und muss beim Schulleiter abgeholt werden.

(m) Oh je, das kann ich mir vorstellen. Aber du musst bei so einem Gerät auch aufpassen!

(f) Ich weiß. Eine Freundin von mir war in der Stadt in einem Café. Sie hat ihr Handy auf dem Tisch liegen gelassen und irgendjemand hat es geklaut. Sie hat alle ihre Fotos und Telefonnummern verloren. Sie war wirklich traurig und ihre Eltern waren sehr sauer auf sie.

(m) Na gut, was machst du am Wochenende?

(f) Ich glaube, wir fahren zu Oma aufs Land und machen eine Wanderung durch den Wald. Am Sonntag habe ich vor, meinen Freund in der Stadt zu treffen. Das muss ich noch mit ihm verabreden! Das kann ich jetzt mit meinem neues Handy tun!

Item 2 (continued)

(m) OK Schatz, dann viel Spaß mit deinem neuen Geschenk. Ich muss los!

(f) Tschüss, ich sag' der Mama, dass du vorbeigekommen bist. Bis bald!

(*2 minutes*)

(t) End of test.
Now look over your answers.

[END OF MODEL TRANSCRIPT]

HIGHER FOR CfE

Model Paper 3

Whilst this Model Practice Paper has been specially commissioned by Hodder Gibson for use as practice for the Higher (for Curriculum for Excellence) exams, the key reference document remains the SQA Specimen Paper 2014.

National Qualifications
MODEL PAPER 3

German Reading

Duration — 1 hour and 40 minutes

Total marks — 30

Attempt ALL questions.

Write your answers clearly, in **English**, in the Reading Answer Booklet provided. In the answer booklet you must clearly identify the question number you are attempting.

You may use a German dictionary.

Use **blue** or **black** ink.

There is a separate question and answer booklet for Directed Writing. You must complete your answer for Directed Writing in the question and answer booklet for Directed Writing.

Before leaving the examination room you must give your Reading answer booklet and your Directed Writing answer booklet to the Invigilator; if you do not, you may lose all the marks for this paper.

Total marks — 30

Read the whole article carefully and then answer, in English, ALL the questions that follow.

The article discusses attitudes to holiday jobs.

Fereinjobs — eine gute Idee?

Markenklamotten, Führerschein, Urlaub mit Freunden — all das kostet viel Geld. Geld, das Schülerinnen und Schülern nicht selbstverständlich haben. Die Lösung: Jobben in den Sommerferien.

Doch wo können Jugendliche auch jetzt noch einen Ferienjob finden? Julia Weber,
5 Mitarbeiterin eines Arbeitsamtes in Nordbayern, behauptet, dass es zahlreiche Möglichkeiten gibt, einen Ferienjob zu finden. Erster Anlaufpunkt könnten die Stellenanzeigen in der regionalen Tageszeitung sein. Auch Eltern, Freunde, Bekannte und Verwandte kennen vielleicht ein Unternehmen, das Ferienjobs anbietet. Weitere Möglichkeiten einen Ferienjob zu finden sind zum Beispiel die schwarzen Bretter in vielen
10 Supermärkten.

<u>Auch ein Schaufensterbummel durch die Innenstadt kann weiterhelfen. Eisdielen, Cafés, Restaurants und viele andere kleine Geschäfte suchen speziell in den Sommerferien nach Aushilfen, die einfache Tätigkeiten machen, für die kein besonderes Vorwissen erforderlich ist.</u>

15 Aber es ist nicht immer so einfach, einen Ferienjob zu finden. Bessere Chancen haben Schüler in Geschäften, sagt Michael Schmitz vom Handelsverband Bayern. „In Geschäften ist die Nachfrage nach Ferienjobs hoch — es gibt mehr Leute als Arbeitsstellen. Gründe hierfür sind beispielsweise die Konkurrenz durch Minijobber mit Berufserfahrung und zum Teil auch die geringe Mobilität von Schülern." Studenten haben normalerweise eine
20 höhere Chance auf einen Ferienjob in einem Geschäft, da sie meist länger zur Verfügung stehen und weniger Arbeitsbedingungen haben. „Jobber unter 18 Jahren werden aber gerne in Lebensmittelgeschäften zum Auffüllen von Regalen angestellt", sagt Schmitz.

Ein Ferienjob bietet für Jugendliche viele Vorteile. Zum einen lässt sich mit einem Ferienjob das eigene Taschengeld aufbessern, so dass sich Schüler auch Sonderwünsche
25 erfüllen können, zum Beispiel, eine neue Spielkonsole oder ein neues Smartphone selbst verdienen. Dies ist wichtig, besonders wenn die Eltern dafür nicht aufkommen wollen oder es aus finanziellen Gründen nicht können. Peter Meier, Besitzer eines Restaurants, meint: „Jugendliche, die sich durch einen Ferienjob ihr eigenes Geld verdienen, lernen außerdem, dass man hart für sein Geld arbeiten muss."

30 Ein weiterer Vorteil für den Jugendlichen ist die Tatsache, dass Ferienjobs eine exzellente Möglichkeit darstellen, um erste Eindrücke von der Arbeitswelt zu bekommen. Für Schüler kann ein Ferienjob die Chance auf einen Ausbildungsplatz erhöhen. Viele Arbeitgeber sind froh, wenn sie Bewerbungen von Schülern erhalten, die bereits Arbeitserfahrung von Ferienjobs oder Praktika haben.

35 Laut der Ergebnisse einer Umfrage hat jeder dritte der befragten Schüler in Köln einen Ferienjob. Sarah, Schülerin eines Kölner Gymnasiums, arbeitet seit anderthalb Monaten als Verkäuferin in einem Modegeschäft in der Stadtmitte. Ihr gefällt die Arbeit: „Ich liebe den Umgang mit Kunden und ich bin jetzt verantwortungsbewusster. Obwohl ich manchmal nach einem langen Tag erschöpft bin und mein Freund sauer ist, da er mich
40 nicht so oft sieht, weiß ich, dass es sich lohnt. In diesem Job verdiene ich ganz gut und ich kann etwas Geld zurücklegen, weil ich nächstes Jahr vorhabe, eine Weltreise zu machen, bevor ich an die Fachhochschule gehe, um BWL* zu studieren."

Auf der anderen Seite machen sich viele Eltern und Lehrer darum Sorgen. Christina Baur, Direktorin einer Realschule, steht Ferienjobs sehr kritisch gegenüber. „Obwohl ein
45 Ferienjob viele Vorteile mit sich bringt, gibt es auch einen negativen Aspekt, den Schüler und ihre Eltern nicht aus den Augen verlieren sollten. Der Ferienjob schränkt die Erholung in den Ferien ein. Diese ist für Schüler, besonders wenn sie einen Schulabschluss vorbereiten, unbedingt erforderlich. Für viele Jugendliche im Alter von 15–18 Jahren ist der Leistungsdruck in der Schule enorm und sie sollten während der Ferien genug Kraft
50 tanken, um auch nach dem Urlaub mit der Schule wieder engagiert anzufangen. Ein Ferienjob kann sich schon nachteilig auf ihre Noten auswirken."

Für Psychologe Michael Stein ist es wichtig, dass man die goldene Mitte findet: „Obwohl man mit einem Ferienjob neue Fähigkeiten entwickeln kann, sollte man auch Zeit für sich haben und vorsichtig sein, dass man nicht ausgenutzt wird."

*BWL = Betriebswirtschaftslehre

MARKS

Questions

Re-read lines 1–10

1. According to the text, school pupils do not have a lot of money. What type of things do they need money for? State any **two** things. **2**

2. According to job centre worker, Julia Weber, what different ways are there to find a job? Give any **two** details. **2**

Re-read lines 15–29

3. Michael Schmitz from the Bavarian Trade Association claims that it is difficult for pupils to get a job in a shop. Why is this? State any **two** things. **2**

4. (a) Why do students have a better chance of getting a job in a shop than school pupils? Give **two** details. **2**

    (b) What kind of work can a young person under the age of 18 do in a grocery shop? State **one** thing. **1**

5. Working during the holidays can give young people many financial advantages.

    (a) What are these advantages? Give any **two** details. **2**

    (b) In what way are holiday jobs important for young people? State **one** thing. **1**

Re-read lines 30–42

6. According to the text, what can holiday jobs provide for young people? Give any **two** details. **2**

MARKS

7. According to the results of a recent survey in Cologne, every third pupil interviewed had a holiday job.

    (a) Sarah enjoys her job. Why is this? State **one** thing.   1

    (b) What does Sarah say are the disadvantages? State **one** thing.   1

    (c) What is Sarah planning to do in the future? State **one** thing.   1

    Re-read lines 53–55

8. Psychologist Michael Stein thinks it is important to find a balance when working during the holidays. Why is this? State **one** thing.   1

9. Now consider the article as a whole. Is the writer positive or negative about young people having a holiday job? Give reasons for your answer with reference to the text.   2

10. Translate into English:

    "Auch ein Schaufensterbummel .... Tätigkeiten machen." (*lines 11–14*)   10

[END OF MODEL QUESTION PAPER]

FOR OFFICIAL USE

National Qualifications
MODEL PAPER 3

Mark

German
Directed Writing

Duration — 1 hour and 40 minutes

Fill in these boxes and read what is printed below.

Full name of centre

Town

Forename(s)

Surname

Number of seat

Date of birth
Day   Month   Year

Scottish candidate number

Total marks — 10

Choose ONE scenario on *Page two* and write your answer clearly, in **German**, in the space provided in this booklet. You must clearly identify the scenario number you are attempting.

You may use a German dictionary.

Additional space for answers is provided at the end of this booklet.

Use **blue** or **black** ink.

There is a separate answer booklet for Reading. You must complete your answers for Reading in the answer booklet for Reading.

Before leaving the examination room you must give this Directed Writing question and answer booklet and your Reading answer booklet to the Invigilator; if you do not, you may lose all the marks for this paper.

Total marks — 10

Choose **one** of the following two scenarios.

SCENARIO 1: Culture

> While visiting your Swiss friend in Zürich, you went to see a play in German at the theatre.
>
> On your return, your German teacher asks you to write **in German** about the experience.

You must include the following information and **you should try to add** other relevant details:

- how you travelled to the theatre **and** what the play was about
- what you liked most about the play
- what you did before the play
- whether you would recommend this experience to a friend

You should write approximately 120–150 words.

OR

SCENARIO 2: Society

> You went on holiday with your family to Germany.
>
> On your return, your teacher asks you to write **in German** about your experience.

You must include the following information and **you should try to add** other relevant details:

- where you went **and** who you went with
- how you got on together
- what you did during your stay
- whether you would recommend going on a family holiday

You should write approximately 120–150 words.

Scenario number

ANSWER SPACE (continued)

ANSWER SPACE (continued)

[END OF MODEL QUESTION PAPER]

ADDITIONAL SPACE FOR ANSWERS

ADDITIONAL SPACE FOR ANSWERS

FOR OFFICIAL USE

National Qualifications
MODEL PAPER 3

Mark

German
Listening and Writing

Duration — 1 hour

Fill in these boxes and read what is printed below.

Full name of centre

Town

Forename(s)

Surname

Number of seat

Date of birth
Day Month Year

Scottish candidate number

Total marks — 30

SECTION 1 — LISTENING — 20 marks
You will hear two items in German. **Before you hear each item, you will have one minute to study the questions.** You will hear each item twice, with an interval of one minute between playings. You will then have time to answer the questions before hearing the next item. Write your answers, in **English**, in the spaces provided.

SECTION 2 — WRITING — 10 marks
Write your answer, in **German**, in the space provided.

Attempt ALL questions. You may use a German dictionary.

Additional space for answers is provided at the end of this booklet. If you use this space you must clearly identify the question number you are attempting.

You are not allowed to leave the examination room until the end of the test.

Use **blue** or **black** ink.

Before leaving the examination room you must give this booklet to the Invigilator; if you do not, you may lose all the marks for this paper.

SECTION 1 — LISTENING — 20 marks

Attempt ALL questions

Item 1

You listen to a German radio report about all-day schools in North Rhine Westphalia.

(a) According to the latest statistics, the number of all-day schools in North Rhine Westphalia has increased. What evidence is there of this? State any **one** thing. **1**

(b) The local government has invested a lot of money in this system. According to the passage, what are the positive aspects of all-day schools? State any **two** things. **2**

(c) There are many critics of the system. What points do they mention? State any **two** things. **2**

(d) According to educational experts, what two factors are required to create a good all-day school? State any **two** things. **2**

(e) Consider the report as a whole. Overall, what does the government think about all-day schools? Tick (✓) the correct statement. **1**

The report highlights that the government is generally negative about all-day schools.	
The report highlights that the government does not want to invest in all-day schools.	
The report highlights that the government is positive about all-day schools.	

Item 2

Thomas speaks to Claudia about her final year at school.

(a) (i) What is Claudia studying for? State **one** thing. **1**

(ii) Claudia is stressed. Why is this? State any **two** things. **2**

(b) Why can Claudia not relax? State any **one** thing. **1**

(c) Claudia talks about the subjects she is studying. What does she say about:

(i) ... biology? State any **two** things. **2**

(ii) ... maths? State any **two** things. **2**

(d) How does Claudia prepare for exams? State any **one** thing. **1**

(e) Claudia talks about going to university in Vienna.

(i) What job would she like to do in the future? State **one** thing. **1**

(ii) What training does she have to complete to do this? State any **two** things. **2**

SECTION 2 — WRITING — 10 marks

Claudia bereitet ihr Abitur vor. Wie ist das mit dir? Welche Fächer lernst du dieses Jahr? Verstehst du dich gut mit deinen Lehrern? Möchtest du studieren oder eine Lehre machen?

Schreibe 120–150 Wörter zu diesen Fragen.

ADDITIONAL SPACE FOR ANSWERS

ADDITIONAL SPACE FOR ANSWERS

National Qualifications MODEL PAPER 3

German
Listening Transcript

Duration — 1 hour

This paper must not be seen by any candidate.

The material overleaf is provided for use in an emergency only (eg the recording or equipment proving faulty) or where permission has been given in advance by SQA for the material to be read to candidates with additional support needs. The material must be read exactly as printed.

Transcript — Higher

> **Instructions to reader(s):**
>
> For each item, read the English **once**, then read the German **twice**, with an interval of 1 minute between the two readings. On completion of the second reading, pause for the length of time indicated in brackets after the item, to allow the candidates to write their answers.
>
> Where special arrangements have been agreed in advance to allow the reading of the material, those sections marked **(f)** should be read by a female speaker and those marked **(m)** by a male; those sections marked **(t)** should be read by the teacher.

(t) **Item 1**

You listen to a German radio report about all-day schools in North Rhine Westphalia.

You now have one minute to study the questions for Item 1.

(m/f) In den letzten Monaten haben Lehrer, Eltern und Schüler das Schulsystem in Nordrhein-Westfalen diskutiert.

Laut einer aktuellen Statistik ist die Anzahl der Gesamtschulen in Nordrhein-Westfalen gestiegen: Jeder vierte Schüler im Bundesland besucht eine der 281 Gesamtschulen. Vor acht Jahren war es nur jeder zehnte.

Die Regierung in Nordrhein-Westfalen hat viel Geld in neue Gesamtschulen investiert und behauptet, dass das System sehr positiv ist. Für Schüler gibt es mehr Angebote an Nebenfächern wie Kunst und Sport und sie haben am Nachmittag Hilfe mit den Hausaufgaben. Sie haben auch die Gelegenheit zusammenzuarbeiten und der Stundenplan ist für jeden Schüler persönlich zusammen gestellt. Eltern die arbeiten, müssen sich keine Sorgen wegen Kinderbetreuung und Mittagessen machen.

Auf der anderen Seite sagen die Kritiker, dass es höhere Kosten für Materialien und Lehrer und weniger Freizeit für Hobbys, Musikschulen und Vereine gibt. Lehrer haben mehr Einfluss auf die Erziehung als die Eltern und Schüler sind müde nach einem langen Tag in der Schule.

Manche Bildungsexperten meinen, dass zwei Faktoren wichtig sind um eine gute Ganztagsschule zu schaffen: Erstens ist das ein guter Stundenplan, der die Schüler nicht überfordert und eine Mischung aus Lernstunden und Erholung anbietet, wie zum Beispiel Sport. Zweitens gilt es, hochmotivierte und qualifizierte Lehrkräfte einzustellen, das heißt, Lehrer, die ihren Job lieben und gern mit Jugendlichen arbeiten.

(*2 minutes*)

(t) **Item 2**

Thomas speaks to Claudia about her final year of school.

You now have one minute to study the questions for Item 2.

(m) **Na, Claudia, wie geht's? Lernst du immer noch?**

(f) Ja, hallo Thomas. Nicht schlecht, ich lerne immer noch für diese Klassenarbeit in Mathe morgen! Ich stehe völlig unter Stress – du nicht?

(m) **Nö, ich nicht. Es ist nur eine blöde Klassenarbeit! Du bist immer so ein Streber!**

(f) Naja, so ist es. Ich muss sie bestehen, sonst sind meine Eltern enttäuscht. Sie sagen mir immer, ohne Fleiß keinen Preis und ich spüre ständig diesen Leistungsdruck, da meine ältere Schwester vor zwei Jahren ein tolles Abitur gemacht hat.

(m) **Sag mal, kannst du nicht wenigstens ein bisschen relaxen?**

(f) Nur ganz selten, höchstens am Wochenende, wenn ich mit mir oder meinem Freund allein bin. Sonst habe ich ein schlechtes Gewissen, weil ich jede Minute zum Lernen nutzen sollte. Ich freue mich schon auf den Sommer!

(m) **Welchen Schwerpunkt hast du dieses Jahr?**

(f) Ich habe den Schwerpunkt Naturwissenschaft. Mein Lieblingsfach ist Biologie, weil es unheimlich interessant aber eklig ist. Ich finde alles faszinierend und die Lehrerin kann sehr gut erklären und das kann ich normalerweise sehr leicht behalten. Mathe, auf der anderen Seite, kann ich gar nicht leiden – der Lehrer ist so monoton und manchmal muss ich selber nachschlagen, weil ich nicht immer verstehe, wie er es erklärt. Außerdem wiederholen wir immer so viel – die gleiche Übung mehrmals zu machen ist total langweilig.

(m) **Damit bin ich total einverstanden! Wie bereitest du dich auf die Prüfungen vor?**

(f) Ich versuche meine Prüfungsvorbereitung zu planen, so dass ich alles schaffe. Ich bin ein visueller Lerner und in meinem Zimmer kleben viele Notizen und Grafiken an der Wand. Auch wichtig für mich ist viel Wasser zu trinken und Sport zu treiben, um den Stress abzubauen.

(m) **Ich fange erst am Abend vor der Prüfung an! Was machst du im Sommer?**

(f) Ja, das überrascht mich gar nicht. Im Sommer fahre ich zehn Tage mit meinem Freund nach Griechenland. Dann muss ich mir überlegen, was das nächste Jahr bringen wird.

(m) **Hast du schon entschieden, was du nächstes Jahr machst?**

(f) Ja, ich glaube schon. Ich habe vor, Chemie an der Uni in Wien zu studieren, da ich Apothekerin werden möchte.

(m) **Ja, klingt toll. Und wie lange dauert das?**

(f) Sehr lange! Nach fünf Jahren an der Uni muss ich ein Jahr lang Praktikum machen und dann noch die Staatsexamen bestehen. Ein Apotheker muss sich immer weiterbilden, da jedes Jahr immer neue Medikamente auf den Markt kommen.

Page three

Item 2 (continued)

(m) Ach du lieber... besser du als ich. Ich werde mit meiner Lehre als Elektroniker zufrieden sein! Sehen wir uns am Wochenende?

(f) Ja, mal sehen... weiß ich noch nicht. Ich ruf' dich später an... jetzt mache ich weiter mit dem Pauken!

(2 minutes)

(t) End of test.

Now look over your answers.

[END OF MODEL TRANSCRIPT]

HIGHER FOR CfE

Model Paper 4

Whilst this Model Practice Paper has been specially commissioned by Hodder Gibson for use as practice for the Higher (for Curriculum for Excellence) exams, the key reference document remains the SQA Specimen Paper 2014.

National Qualifications
MODEL PAPER 4

German Reading

Duration — 1 hour and 40 minutes

Total marks — 30

Attempt ALL questions.

Write your answers clearly, in **English**, in the Reading Answer Booklet provided. In the answer booklet you must clearly identify the question number you are attempting.

You may use a German dictionary.

Use **blue** or **black** ink.

There is a separate question and answer booklet for Directed Writing. You must complete your answer for Directed Writing in the question and answer booklet for Directed Writing.

Before leaving the examination room you must give your Reading answer booklet and your Directed Writing answer booklet to the Invigilator; if you do not, you may lose all the marks for this paper.

Total marks — 30

Read the whole article carefully and then answer, in English, ALL the questions that follow.

The article discusses a recent visit to Scotland by a German teenager.

Shottland — ein Land, ganz anders, als wir es uns vorstellen!

Etwas Neues zu erleben, Freunde aus aller Welt zu finden und in einer Familie, die im ersten Augenblick fremd ist, einen Platz zu finden — das waren meine Erwartungen an meine Zeit im Ausland. Ohne lange überlegt zu haben, stand für mich fest: Nach Schottland sollte es gehen!

5 Auch wenn Schottland nicht als „das Land der unbegrenzten Möglichkeiten" bekannt ist, nicht im Regenwald liegt und das Wetter nun auch nicht immer so gut ist, haben mich der bekannte Humor der Schotten und die typische schottische Lebensweise gereizt. Manche meiner Freunden meinten zu mir: „Schottland — darüber haben wir doch schon so oft im Unterricht gesprochen!" Darauf kann ich jetzt antworten: „Schottland ist ganz anders, als
10 wir es uns vorstellen!"

Andere Länder, andere Sitten

Natürlich ist bekannt, dass in Schottland die Autos auf der anderen Straßenseite fahren, doch sich daran zu gewöhnen, als Mitfahrer auf der „deutschen" Fahrerseite eines Autos einzusteigen, braucht ein wenig Zeit. Des Weiteren ist Schottland ja für seine „tea time"
15 berühmt. Früher stellte ich mir darunter Folgendes vor: Eine Familie sitzt friedlich um 5.00 Uhr nachmittags zusammen, trinkt Tee und isst Kuchen. Doch gleich in der ersten Woche fiel mir auf: Da ist nichts mit Kuchen und Tee. Mit „tea" ist eine vollwertige warme Mahlzeit gemeint, weil mittags nur ein Pausenbrot gegessen wird, bestehend aus Sandwich, Chips, einer Tomate und Keksen.

20 ### „Ganztagsschule" - gar nicht so schlimm

Bereits an meinem zweiten Tag in Edinburgh hatte ich meinen ersten Schultag. Ich wusste, dass es in Schottland ausschließlich Ganztagsschulen gibt. Also stellte ich mir vor, dass ich mit acht bzw. zehn Schulstunden rechnen musste. Der Tag war viel kürzer als ich erwartet habe. Ein normaler Schultag beginnt aber erst um 9.00 Uhr. Der Schultag
25 beinhaltet sechs Schulstunden, die jeweils 50 Minuten dauern. Somit ging ein Schultag um 15.00 Uhr schon wieder zu Ende. Das ist doch fast wie Ferien!

Interessante Fächerauswahl

Die schottische Oberstufe unterscheidet sich deutlich von der Oberstufe an deutschen Schulen. Jeder Schüler hat bis fünf Fächer, die den Leistungskursen in unserem
30 Schulsystem gleichen. Neben den „normalen" Schulfächern wie Chemie und Geschichte werden zum Beispiel auch Reisen und Tourismus und Psychologie angeboten. Bei der großen und interessanten Auswahl fiel mir die Entscheidung zunächst schwer.

In den kleinen Kursen findet man schnell neue Freunde

Die Oberstufe meiner Schule war ziemlich klein. Entsprechend klein waren auch unsere
35 Kurse. Damit diese außergewöhnlichen Fächer zu Stande kommen konnten, gab es die Möglichkeit, Fächer an einer anderen Schule im Ort zu belegen. So kam es, dass mein Musikunterricht an der Partnerschule stattfand. Diese kleinen Kurse waren eine gute Möglichkeit, neue Freunde zu finden. So entwickelte sich zwischen mir und meinen beiden Mitschülern aus dem Musikkurs, Tim und Hannah, eine feste Freundschaft.

40 **Der nächste Schottland-Besuch ist sicher**

Nach einem unvergesslichen Weihnachtsfest und einem aufregenden Silvester mit meiner schottischen Familie, einem lustigen Abend im Kino mit anschließendem Pizzaessen zum Abschied mit meinen besten Freunden, machte ich mich wieder auf den Weg in Richtung Deutschland. Einige Tränen flossen, als mir endgültig bewusst wurde, dass meine Zeit in
45 Schottland nur begrenzt war. Doch konnte ich allen versprechen, dass es sich nur um einen Abschied auf Zeit handelte, denn schon in den darauf folgenden Sommerferien verbrachte ich wieder einige Zeit in meiner britischen Heimat. Ich bin mir sicher, dass noch zahlreiche weitere Besuche folgen werden.

Mit Klischees aufgeräumt – und eine zweite Heimat gefunden

50 <u>Ich bereue meine Entscheidung kein bisschen, Deutschland für eine Zeit verlassen zu haben. Es ist eine tolle Erfahrung, ich habe in Edinburgh eine zweite Heimat gefunden. Sich neu zu orientieren, kostet Zeit, aber das ist es wert.</u> Es ist ein schönes Gefühl, an zwei Orten zur gleichen Zeit immer lieb aufgenommen zu werden. Während meiner Zeit dort habe ich viel über das schottische Leben gelernt und viele Klischees hinter mir
55 gelassen, denn Schottland ist eben „ein Land, ganz anders, als wir es uns vorstellen!"

Questions

MARKS

Re-read lines 1–10

1. What expectations did the writer have before going abroad? State any **two** things. 2

2. The writer gives reasons for visiting Scotland. What are they? Give **two** details. 2

Re-read lines 12–19

3. Different countries have different customs.

   (a) What did the writer have to get used to when travelling by car? State any **one** thing. 1

   (b) Scotland is famous for its teatime. In what way was her perception of teatime different to the reality? State any **two** things. 2

Re-read lines 21–39

4. The writer visited an all-day school in Edinburgh.

   (a) What was her experience of the school day? Give any **two** details. 2

   (b) What subjects could she study alongside the 'normal' subjects? State **two** things. 1

   (c) What did she think about the choice of subjects offered? State **one** thing. 1

MARKS

5. The writer tells us that the class sizes were very small.

    (a) What had to happen as a result of this? State **one** thing. 1

    (b) Why did she enjoy this? State **one** thing. 1

    Re-read lines 41–55

6. (a) When did the writer return to Germany? Give any **two** details. 2

    (b) What were her feelings about leaving? Give any **two** details. 2

7. The writer has a better understanding of Scotland. In what way has she achieved this? State any **one** thing. 1

8. Now consider the article as a whole. Was the writer's experience of Scotland positive or negative? Give reasons for your answer with reference to the text. 2

9. Translate into English:

    "Ich bereue .... es wert." (*lines 50–53*) 10

[END OF MODEL QUESTION PAPER]

FOR OFFICIAL USE

National Qualifications
MODEL PAPER 4

H

Mark

German
Directed Writing

Duration — 1 hour and 40 minutes

Fill in these boxes and read what is printed below.

Full name of centre

Town

Forename(s)

Surname

Number of seat

Date of birth
Day   Month   Year

Scottish candidate number

Total marks — 10

Choose ONE scenario on *Page two* and write your answer clearly, in **German**, in the space provided in this booklet. You must clearly identify the scenario number you are attempting.

You may use a German dictionary.

Additional space for answers is provided at the end of this booklet.

Use **blue** or **black** ink.

There is a separate answer booklet for Reading. You must complete your answers for Reading in the answer booklet for Reading.

Before leaving the examination room you must give this Directed Writing question and answer booklet and your Reading answer booklet to the Invigilator; if you do not, you may lose all the marks for this paper.

Total marks — 10

Choose **one** of the following two scenarios.

SCENARIO 1: Society

> Last month, you went on a school trip to Berlin to visit the German parliament.
>
> On your return, your German teacher asks you to write **in German** about the experience.

You must include the following information and **you should try to add** other relevant details:

- how you travelled **and** where you stayed
- what you thought of the German parliament
- what you did in your spare time
- whether you would return to Berlin

You should write approximately 120–150 words.

OR

SCENARIO 2: Learning

> Last week, your partner school from München visited your school.
>
> As part of the project, your teacher asks you to write **in German** about your experience.

You must include the following information and **you should try to add** other relevant details:

- how your exchange partner travelled to Scotland **and** what they did when they arrived
- how s/he got on with your family
- what you did in the evenings
- whether you would recommend taking part in an exchange

You should write approximately 120–150 words.

Scenario number

ANSWER SPACE (continued)

ANSWER SPACE (continued)

ANSWER SPACE (continued)

[END OF MODEL QUESTION PAPER]

ADDITIONAL SPACE FOR ANSWERS

ADDITIONAL SPACE FOR ANSWERS

National Qualifications
MODEL PAPER 4

Mark

German
Listening and Writing

Duration — 1 hour

Fill in these boxes and read what is printed below.

Full name of centre

Town

Forename(s)

Surname

Number of seat

Date of birth
Day Month Year

Scottish candidate number

Total marks — 30

SECTION 1 — LISTENING — 20 marks

You will hear two items in German. **Before you hear each item, you will have one minute to study the questions.** You will hear each item twice, with an interval of one minute between playings. You will then have time to answer the questions before hearing the next item. Write your answers, in **English**, in the spaces provided.

SECTION 2 — WRITING — 10 marks

Write your answer, in **German**, in the space provided.

Attempt ALL questions. You may use a German dictionary.

Additional space for answers is provided at the end of this booklet. If you use this space you must clearly identify the question number you are attempting.

You are not allowed to leave the examination room until the end of the test.

Use **blue** or **black** ink.

Before leaving the examination room you must give this booklet to the Invigilator; if you do not, you may lose all the marks for this paper.

SECTION 1 — LISTENING — 20 marks

Attempt ALL questions

Item 1

You listen to a German radio report about young people working part-time in Germany.

(a) A new study has shown a considerable number of young people working. What evidence is there of this? State any **one** thing. **1**

(b) The law protecting young people regulates the working conditions and hours.

　(i) How many hours are 13–15 year olds allowed to work? **1**

　(ii) Young people can do certain types of jobs only. What jobs are they? State any **two** things. **2**

(c) According to employers and parents, why is it important that young people have the right to work? State any **two** things. **2**

(d) What do teachers recommend? State any **one** thing. **1**

(e) Consider the report as a whole. Overall, what does the report say about young people working? Tick (✓) the correct statement. **1**

The report is mostly positive about the impact of part-time work.	
The report does not recommend that young people work.	
The report is mostly critical about the impact of part-time work.	

Page two

Item 2

Anna speaks to Moritz about his part-time job.

(a) Moritz works part-time.

    (i) Where exactly does he work? **1**

    (ii) How long has he been working there? **1**

(b) What did he do to get the job? State any **two** things. **2**

(c) Moritz talks about his tasks at work. What exactly does he have to do? Give any **two** details. **2**

(d) Anna thinks his job is a lot of work. What is Moritz's response? State any **two** things. **2**

(e) How does he get on with his colleagues? State any **two** things. **2**

(f) Moritz then talks about money.

    (i) What does he say about his pocket money? Give any **one** detail. **1**

    (ii) How does he feel about this? Give any **one** detail. **1**

SECTION 2 — WRITING — 10 marks

Moritz hat über seinen Teilzeitjob gesprochen. Wie ist das mit dir? Hast du einen Nebenjob? Musst du zu Hause im Haushalt helfen? Was sind die Vor- und Nachteile, wenn man einen Nebenjob hat?

Schreibe 120–150 Wörter zu diesen Fragen.

[END OF MODEL QUESTION PAPER]

ADDITIONAL SPACE FOR ANSWERS

ADDITIONAL SPACE FOR ANSWERS

National Qualifications
MODEL PAPER 4

German
Listening Transcript

Duration — 1 hour

This paper must not be seen by any candidate.

The material overleaf is provided for use in an emergency only (eg the recording or equipment proving faulty) or where permission has been given in advance by SQA for the material to be read to candidates with additional support needs. The material must be read exactly as printed.

Transcript — Higher

Instructions to reader(s):

For each item, read the English **once**, then read the German **twice**, with an interval of 1 minute between the two readings. On completion of the second reading, pause for the length of time indicated in brackets after the item, to allow the candidates to write their answers.

Where special arrangements have been agreed in advance to allow the reading of the material, those sections marked **(f)** should be read by a female speaker and those marked **(m)** by a male; those sections marked **(t)** should be read by the teacher.

(t) Item 1

You listen to a German radio report about young people working part-time in Germany.

You now have one minute to study the questions for Item 1.

(m/f) Sozialarbeiter und Lehrer haben in den letzten Wochen die Situation der Jugendarbeit diskutiert.

Eine neue Studie zeigt, dass die Anzahl an Schülern, die einen Teilzeitjob haben, weiter steigt. Jeder zehnte Schüler geht neben der Schule arbeiten und gut die Hälfte der Schüler arbeitet während den Sommerferien.

Ein Gesetz regelt die Arbeitsstunden und Arbeitsbedingungen der Jugendlichen. Bis zum 13. Lebensjahr ist das Arbeiten komplett verboten und danach dürfen 13 bis 15-Jährige nur zwei Stunden pro Tag mit der Zustimmung der Eltern arbeiten. Allerdings dürfen sie nur leichte Tätigkeiten ausüben, zum Beispiel mit Hunden spazieren gehen, Nachhilfe geben, Zeitungen austragen oder Gartenarbeit machen.

Viele Arbeitgeber und Eltern sind damit einverstanden, dass Jugendliche das Recht auf einen Teilzeitjob haben. Sie meinen, dass Jugendliche lernen mit Geld umzugehen und finanzielle Verantwortung zu übernehmen. Jugendliche die arbeiten, verstehen den Wert von Geld besser und bekommen einen Einblick in die Welt der Arbeit. Sie lernen dadurch auch neue Eigenschaften, wie Pünktlichkeit, Organisation und Selbstvertrauen.

Außerdem glauben viele Lehrer, dass Arbeit gut für die Entwicklung der Disziplin der Schüler ist. Sie empfehlen auch freiwillige Arbeit, wenn diese keinen schlechten Einfluss auf die Schularbeit hat.

Die deutsche Regierung muss alles tun, um Jugendliche in der Arbeitswelt zu schützen. Obwohl Berufserfahrung wichtig für den zukünftigen Erfolg ist, muss man immer daran denken, dass die Gesundheit an erster Stelle steht.

(2 minutes)

(t) **Item 2**

Anna speaks to Moritz about his part-time job.

You now have one minute to study the questions for Item 2.

(f) Servus, Moritz! Hast du Lust am Freitagnachmittag mit mir ins Schwimmbad zu gehen?

(m) Hallo, Anna. Ich würde gern mit dir dorthin gehen, aber ich kann nicht. Tut mir Leid, ich arbeite direkt nach der Schule.

(f) Ach so, schade! Wo arbeitest du nochmal?

(m) Ich arbeite als Kellner im kleinen italienischen Restaurant in der Stadtmitte. Kennst du doch — gleich gegenüber der Sparkasse. Ich arbeite dort seit anderthalb Jahren.

(f) Ah ja, ich weiß genau wo das ist. Wie hast du den Job gefunden?

(m) Mein Vater kennt die Frau des Besitzers. Er hat sie gefragt, ob es irgendeine freie Stelle gibt. Ich musste ein Bewerbungsformular online ausfüllen, und auch einen Lebenslauf schicken. Danach bekam ich ein Vorstellungsgespräch und dann eine vierwöchige Probezeit und Schulung. Bevor ich allein arbeiten durfte, musste ich ein Gesundheitszeugnis bestehen.

(f) Cool, und was sind jetzt deine Aufgaben?

(m) Naja, es kommt drauf an. Normalerweise nehme ich Bestellungen von den Gästen auf und ich habe auch die Speisekarte auswendig gelernt, damit ich ihre Fragen beantworten kann. Ich bin froh, dass ich ein bisschen Italienisch in der Schule gelernt habe, da es bei Empfehlungen hilft. Ich muss die Bestellungen in den Computer eintippen, die Getränke vorbereiten und servieren. Ich muss auch kassieren und abrechnen und wenn die Gäste das Restaurant verlassen, decke ich den Tisch neu.

(f) Oh je, klingt nach viel Arbeit?

(m) Ach es geht noch. Weil wir ständig arbeiten, vergeht die Zeit schnell. Aber es stimmt, manchmal bin ich morgens hundemüde in der Schule und die Lehrer beschweren sich, wenn ich meine Hausaufgaben nicht mache. Sie verstehen einfach nicht, dass ich nicht alles kann. Trotzdem ist das Gehalt sehr gut für Jugendliche und wir dürfen unser Trinkgeld behalten. Außerdem habe ich viele neue Fertigkeiten entwickelt, die man in der Schule nicht lernen kann. Also ich kann nicht klagen.

(f) Was zum Beispiel?

(m) Man muss sehr gut mit Geld und Kunden umgehen können. Man muss flexibel sein und schnell Lösungen finden, wenn die Gäste nicht zufrieden sind. Deswegen ist es wichtig, kundenorientiert zu sein, das heißt, freundlich und hilfsbereit. Man muss gut zuhören und alles genau aufschreiben.

(f) Und kommst du gut mit den anderen Mitarbeitern aus?

(m) Im Großen und Ganzen verstehen wir uns ziemlich gut, aber manchmal gibt es Krach zwischen den Mitarbeitern — aber das ist doch normal, wenn man unter Druck arbeitet. Wichtig ist, dass wir als Team zusammenarbeiten.

(f) Was machst du mit deinem Geld?

Item 2 (continued)

(m) Tja, da ich kein Taschengeld von meinen Eltern kriege, muss ich alles selber kaufen. Nein, das stimmt nicht — meine Eltern bezahlen alles, was ich brauche, z.B. Klamotten, Schulsachen usw. — den Rest bezahle ich mit meinem Lohn. Ich finde das gerecht, da ich unabhängig von ihnen bin und ich kann mein Geld ausgeben, wie ich möchte.

(f) **Ach meine Mama ruft mich an, wollen wir nächstes Wochenende etwas unternehmen?**

(m) Ja, klar... ich melde mich morgen. Servus!

(2 minutes)

(t) **End of test.**

Now look over your answers.

[END OF MODEL TRANSCRIPT]

HIGHER FOR CfE | ANSWER SECTION

ANSWER SECTION FOR
SQA AND HODDER GIBSON HIGHER FOR CfE GERMAN 2014

HIGHER FOR CfE GERMAN SPECIMEN QUESTION PAPER

Reading

Question		Expected Answer(s)	Max mark
1		• Smartphones, notebooks and tablets are /Technology is part of everyday life for teenagers (in Germany) • It plays an important role in learning	2
2		• Before, a lot of effort was involved or he had to set up the technology in his classroom • Before, he had to go to a computer room • Nowadays there is a whiteboard in every classroom • Nowadays a film presentation is only a few clicks away • (There must be a comparison between then and now) *Any 3 points from possible 5 for 3 marks*	3
3		• Smartphones and computers can make children passive/inactive • Children only deal with information in a superficial way • Computers make pupils addicted *Any 2 points from possible 3 for 2 marks*	2
4		• Using media is (often) a time waster • Teachers experience technical problems • The form is more important than the content *Any 2 points from possible 3 for 2 marks*	2
5		• Each school (he knows) has a different amount of technical equipment / it varies from school to school • His own (grammar) school is not bad • Many schools cannot afford to provide the newest machines/computers	3
6		• Only 4% of parents consider the use of computers in schools to be excellent • In only one in ten schools does every pupil have access to a computer in lessons • Only every third pupil uses computers once a week • 30% of pupils do not use computers in lessons at all *Any 3 points from possible 4 for 3 marks*	3
7		• Pupils should be allowed to use their own computers / machines / devices	1
8		• Teachers have a stressful daily routine • They don't have the time to keep up with current developments in technology	2

Question		Expected Answer(s)	Max mark
9		Outline of possible answers: The writer is mostly negative for the following reasons: • He quotes from people (teachers, academics, politicians and pupils) who give a negative view • He says that Germany is behind other countries • He quotes statistics that demonstrate this • He contrasts Germany's economic success with the lack of technology available in schools	3
10	1	• In general the survey results for teachers are not very good	2
	2	• About half of all pupils	2
	3	• Evaluate the teachers' competence at using media as negative	2
	4	• Every third pupil described their teachers' knowledge of computers as lacking	2
	5	• Most teachers only use hardware and software to show films or presentations	2

Directed Writing

Candidates will write a piece of extended writing in German addressing a scenario that has four related bullet points. Candidates must address each bullet point. The first bullet point contains two pieces of information to be addressed. The remaining three bullet points contain one piece of information each. There is a choice of two scenarios and learners must choose one of these.

Mark	Content	Accuracy	Language resource: variety, range, structures
10	<ul><li>The content is comprehensive</li><li>All bullet points are addressed fully and some candidates may also provide additional relevant information</li></ul>	<ul><li>The language is accurate in all four bullets However, where the candidate attempts to go beyond the range of the task, a slightly higher number of inaccuracies need not detract from the overall very good impression</li><li>A comprehensive range of verbs is used accurately and tenses are consistent and accurate</li><li>There is evidence of confident handling of all aspects of grammar and accurate spelling, although the language may contain a number of minor errors, or even one serious error</li></ul>	<ul><li>The language used is detailed and complex</li><li>There is good use of adjectives, adverbs, prepositional phrases and, where appropriate, word order</li><li>A comprehensive range of verbs/verb forms, tenses and constructions is used</li><li>Some modal verbs and infinitives may be used</li><li>The candidate is comfortable with the first person of the verb and generally uses a different verb in each sentence</li><li>Sentences are mainly complex and accurate</li><li>The language flows well</li></ul>
8	<ul><li>The content is clear</li><li>All bullet points are addressed clearly. The response to one bullet point may be thin, although other bullet points are dealt with in some detail</li></ul>	<ul><li>The language is mostly accurate. Where the candidate attempts to use detailed and complex language, this may be less successful, although basic structures are used accurately</li><li>A range of verbs is used accurately and tenses are generally consistent and accurate</li><li>There may be a few errors in spelling, adjective endings and, where relevant, case endings. Use of accents is less secure, where relevant</li></ul>	<ul><li>The language used is detailed and complex</li><li>In one bullet point the language may be more basic than might otherwise be expected at this level</li><li>The candidate uses a range of verbs/verb forms and other constructions</li><li>There may be less variety in the verbs used</li><li>The candidate is comfortable with the first person of the verb and generally uses a different verb in each sentence</li><li>Sentences are generally complex and mainly accurate</li><li>Overall the writing will be very competent, essentially correct, but may be pedestrian</li></ul>

ANSWERS TO HIGHER FOR CfE GERMAN

Mark	Content	Accuracy	Language resource: variety, range, structures
6	- The content is adequate and may be similar to that of an 8 - Bullet points may be addressed adequately, however **one** of the bullet points may not be addressed	- The language may be mostly accurate in two or three bullet points. However, in the remaining one or two, control of the language structure may deteriorate significantly - The verbs are generally correct, but basic - Tenses may be inconsistent, with present tenses being used at times instead of past tenses - There may be errors in spelling, adjective endings and some prepositions may be inaccurate or omitted. There are quite a few errors in other parts of speech — personal pronouns, gender of nouns, adjective endings, cases (where relevant), singular/plural confusion — and in the use of accents (where relevant) - Overall, there is more correct than incorrect and there is the impression that the candidate can handle tenses	- There are some examples of detailed and complex language - The language is perhaps repetitive and uses a limited range of verbs and fixed phrases not appropriate to this level - The candidate relies on a limited range of vocabulary and structures - There is minimal use of adjectives, probably mainly after "is" - The candidate has a limited knowledge of plurals - A limited range of verbs is used to address some of the bullet points - The candidate copes with the past tense of some verbs - When using the perfect tense, the past participle is incorrect or the auxiliary verb is omitted on occasion - Sentences are mainly single clause and may be brief
4	- The content may be limited and the Directed Writing may be presented as a single paragraph - Bullet points may be addressed in a limited way - **Two** of the bullet points are not be addressed	- The language is mainly inaccurate and after the first bullet the control of the language structure may deteriorate significantly. - A limited range of verbs is used - Ability to form tenses is inconsistent - In the use of the perfect tense the auxiliary verb is omitted on a number of occasions - There may be confusion between the singular and plural form of verbs - There are errors in many other parts of speech — gender of nouns, cases, singular/plural confusion — and in spelling and, where appropriate, word order - Several errors are serious, perhaps showing mother tongue interference	- There is limited use of detailed and complex language - The language is repetitive, with undue reliance on fixed phrases and a limited range of common basic verbs such as to be, to have, to play, to watch - The candidate mainly copes only with simple language - The verbs "was" and "went" may also be used correctly - Sentences are basic and there may be one sentence that is not intelligible to a sympathetic native speaker - An English word may appear in the writing or a word may be omitted - There may be an example of serious dictionary misuse
2	- The content may be basic or similar to that of a 4 or even a 6 - Bullet points are addressed with difficulty.	- The language is inaccurate in all four bullets and there is little control of language structure - Many of the verbs are incorrect or even omitted. There is little evidence of tense control - There are many errors in other parts of speech — personal pronouns, gender of nouns, cases, singular/plural confusion, prepositions, for instance	- There is little use, if any, of detailed and complex language - Verbs used more than once may be written differently on each occasion - The candidate displays almost no knowledge of the past tense of verbs - The candidate cannot cope with more than one or two basic verbs - Sentences are very short and some sentences may not be understood by a sympathetic native speaker

Mark	Content	Accuracy	Language resource: variety, range, structures
0	• The content is very basic • The candidate is unable to address the bullet points Or • **Three or more** of the bullet points are not be addressed	• The language is seriously inaccurate in all four bullets and there is almost no control of language structure • Most errors are serious • Virtually nothing is correct • Very little is intelligible to a sympathetic native speaker	• There is no evidence of detailed and complex language • The candidate may only cope with the verbs to have and to be • There may be several examples of mother tongue interference. • English words are used • Very few words are written correctly in the modern language • There may be several examples of serious dictionary misuse

Section 1 — Listening

Item 1

Question			Expected Answer(s)	Max mark
1	a		• Nearly 50% of young people have siblings • Every fifth child has two siblings *Any 1 point from possible 2 for 1 mark*	1
1	b		• They cannot find a place in a nursery/kindergarten • They must stay at home with the child • They cannot go out to work *Any 2 points from possible 3 for 2 mark*	2
1	c		• The mother has a university degree • The mother has a professional career • The mother earns more money *Any 2 points from possible 3 for 2 marks*	2
1	d	i	• Families will receive financial help	1
1	d	ii	• Every child aged 3 should have a place in nursery/kindergarten • There will be more full-day schools / school day will be longer (so they are not at home alone) *Any 1 point from possible 2 for 1 mark*	1
1	e		• The report highlights some positive changes and some ongoing difficulties	1

Item 2

Question			Expected Answer(s)	Max mark
2	a		• Her mother has remarried • She now has a step brother *Any 1 point from possible 2 for 1 mark*	1
2	b		• Markus is five years younger than Bianca • They have different interests • Markus only talks about tennis • Bianca is not interested in sport • Bianca prefers going to the cinema or (pop) concerts with friends *Any 3 points from possible 5 for 3 marks*	3
2	c		• One weekend they all go to the tennis club / they watch a tennis match • The other weekend they all go to the cinema	2
2	d	i	• Both parents work • Markus's father often works the late shift	2
2	d	ii	• Markus does the vacuuming • Bianca does the dishwasher and / or washing machine • Both walk the dog together • They must tidy their own rooms *Any 2 points from possible 4 for 2 marks*	2
2	e		• It is cool to have a big family/siblings • There is always someone there to talk to (when there is a problem) • She is very glad to have a step-brother *Any 2 points from possible 3 for 2 marks*	2

Section 2 — Writing

Candidates will write 120–150 words in a piece of extended writing in German addressing a stimulus of three questions in German.

Mark	Content	Accuracy	Language resource: variety, range, structures
10	- The content is comprehensive - The topic is addressed fully, in a balanced way - Some candidates may also provide additional information - Overall this comes over as a competent, well thought-out response to the task which reads naturally	- The language is accurate throughout. However where the candidate attempts to go beyond the range of the task, a slightly higher number of inaccuracies need not detract from the overall very good impression - A comprehensive range of verbs is used accurately and tenses are consistent and accurate - There is evidence of confident handling of all aspects of grammar and spelling accurately, although the language may contain a number of minor errors, or even one serious major error	- The language used is detailed and complex - There is good use of adjectives, adverbs, prepositional phrases and, where appropriate, word order - A comprehensive range of verbs/verb forms, tenses and constructions is used - Some modal verbs and infinitives may be used - The candidate is comfortable with the first person of the verb and generally uses a different verb in each sentence - The candidate uses co-ordinating conjunctions and subordinate clauses throughout the writing - Sentences are mainly complex and accurate - The language flows well
8	- The content is clear - The topic is addressed clearly	- The language is mostly accurate. However where the candidate attempts to use detailed and complex language, this may be less successful, although basic structures are used accurately - A range of verbs is used accurately and tenses are generally consistent and accurate - There may be a few errors in spelling, adjective endings and, where relevant, case endings. Use of accents is less secure. - Verbs and other parts of speech are used accurately but simply.	The language used is detailed and complex - The candidate uses a range of verbs/verb forms and other constructions - There may be less variety in the verbs used - The candidate is comfortable with the first person of the verb and generally uses a different verb in each sentence - Most of the more complex sentences use co-ordinating conjunctions, and there may also be examples of subordinating conjunctions where appropriate - Sentences are generally complex and mainly accurate - At times the language may be more basic than might otherwise be expected at this level - There may be an example of minor misuse of dictionary - Overall the writing will be very competent, essentially correct, but may be pedestrian

Mark	Content	Accuracy	Language resource: variety, range, structures
6	• The content is adequate and may be similar to that of an 8 or a 10 • The topic is addressed adequately	• The language may be mostly accurate. However, in places, control of the language structure may deteriorate significantly • The verbs are generally correct, but basic. Tenses may be inconsistent, with present tenses being used at times instead of past tenses • There may be errors in spelling, e.g. reversal of vowel combinations adjective endings and some prepositions may be inaccurate or omitted, e.g. I went the town. There are quite a few errors in other parts of speech – personal pronouns, gender of nouns, adjective endings, cases, singular/plural confusion – and in the use of accents • Overall, there is more correct than incorrect and there is the impression that the candidate can handle tenses	• There are some examples of detailed and complex language • The language is perhaps repetitive and uses a limited range of verbs and fixed phrases not appropriate to this level • The candidate relies on a limited range of vocabulary and structures • There is minimal use of adjectives, probably mainly after "is" • The candidate has a limited knowledge of plurals • The candidate copes with the present tense of most verbs • Where the candidate attempts constructions with modal verbs, these are not always successful • Sentences are mainly single clause and may be brief • There may be some dictionary misuse
4	• The content may be limited and may be presented as a single paragraph • The topic is addressed in a limited way	• The language used to address the more predictable aspects of the task may be accurate. However, major errors occur when the candidate attempts to address a less predictable aspect • A limited range of verbs is used • Ability to form tenses is inconsistent • In the use of the perfect tense the auxiliary verb is omitted on a number of occasions • There may be confusion between the singular and plural form of verbs • There are errors in many other parts of speech – gender of nouns, cases, singular/plural confusion – and in spelling and, where appropriate, word order • Several errors are serious, perhaps showing mother tongue interference • Overall there is more incorrect than correct	• There is limited use of detailed and complex language and the language is mainly simple and predictable • The language is repetitive, with undue reliance on fixed phrases and a limited range of common basic verbs such as to be, to have, to play, to watch • There is inconsistency in the use of various expressions, especially verbs • Sentences are basic and there may be one sentence that is not intelligible to a sympathetic native speaker • An English word may appear in the writing or a word may be omitted • There may be an example of serious dictionary misuse
2	• The content may be basic or similar to that of a 4 or even a 6 • The topic is thinly addressed	• The language is almost completely inaccurate throughout the writing and there is little control of language structure • Many of the verbs are incorrect or even omitted. There is little evidence of tense control • There are many errors in other parts of speech – personal pronouns, gender of nouns, cases, singular/plural confusion • Prepositions are not used correctly	• There is little use, if any, of detailed and complex language • The candidate has a very limited vocabulary • Verbs used more than once may be written differently on each occasion • The candidate cannot cope with more than one or two basic verbs • Sentences are very short and some sentences may not be understood by a sympathetic native speaker • Several English or "made-up" words may appear in the writing • There are examples of serious dictionary misuse

Mark	Content	Accuracy	Language resource: variety, range, structures
0	• The content is very basic • The candidate is unable to address the topic	• The language is seriously inaccurate throughout the writing and there is almost no control of language structure • (Virtually) nothing is correct • Most of the errors are serious • Very little is intelligible to a sympathetic native speaker	• There is no evidence of detailed and complex language • The candidate copes only with "have" and "am" • There may be several examples of mother tongue interference • Very few words are written correctly in the modern language • English words are used • There may be several examples of serious dictionary misuse

# HIGHER FOR CfE GERMAN MODEL PAPER 1

Reading

Question		Expected Answer(s)	Max mark
1	a	• Around 46 million citizens speak a minority language (with great pride) • Many minority languages have already (quietly) died out	2
	b	• Spoken by fewer and fewer people • No longer taught in schools	2
2		• A particular/specific custom • A long history • A unique culture *Any 2 points from possible 3 for 2 marks*	2
3		• Financially supported by national government(s) • Used as the language (of instruction) in schools • Can be seen on bilingual (street) signs • Can be seen in city centres *Any 2 points from possible 4 for 2 marks*	2
4		• Threatened (with extinction) • The governments of Schleswig-Holstein and Mecklenburg-Vorpommern are doing everything to protect the language	2
5	a	• Around 15 children sit in a circle • (Kindergarten) teacher/(nusery) nurse reads the story out loud • The (kindergarten) teacher/(nusery) nurse encourages the children to repeat it *Any 2 points from possible 3 for 2 marks*	2
	b	• The nursery school has been bilingual for more than 10 years	1
6	a	• Breakfast • Washing hands • Making things/handicrafts *Any 1 point from possible 3 for 1 mark*	1
	b	• She uses cards with symbols drawn on • She asks the children what things are called, e.g. chair, cupboard, scissors *Any 1 point from possible 2 for 1 mark*	1

7		• They get used to the language quickly
		• If they do not understand:
		  • another pupil translates
		  • the (kindergarten) teacher/(nusery) nurse explains using gestures and mimes
		Any 1 point from possible 3 for 1 mark
			1

8		• People do not want/do not need the language anymore • Parents think that their children will have no understanding of High German (later) *Any 1 point from possible 2 for 1 mark*	1

Question		Expected Answer(s)	Max mark
9		• Children who grow up with Low German have a better awareness of High German	1
10		Outline of possible answers: The writer has a mixed view for the following reasons: • He acknowledges the decline in minority languages in Europe • He says that many experts claim that many are dying out, too little is being done to protect languages • On the other hand, he cites examples where the language is thriving, that governments are investing in minority languages, and mentions many examples of bilingualism in daily life • He says that many schools are using minority languages	2
11	1	• That is why Andreas has signed up for a language course	2
	2	• at the local (community) college / adult education centre	2
	3	• and looked for private tutors / private teachers in the village.	2
	4	• Today, he even sometimes delivers/conducts/performs his church service in Low German	2
	5	• and says that he has learnt to really appreciate the language.	2

Directed Writing

Please refer back to p142–144 for further advice on the General Marking Principles for Higher German Directed Writing.

Section 1 — Listening

Item 1

Question		Expected Answer(s)	Max mark
1	a	• In the first half of the year, 17 million (foreign) tourists (from abroad) visited Germany • 7% increase on last year *Any 1 point from possible 2 for 1 mark*	1
1	b	• Long history • Rich culture • Cologne/Köln cathedral • The Alps *Any 2 points from possible 4 for 2 marks*	2
1	c	• Cheaper than other European destinations • Tourists feel safe • World-class transport links *Any 2 points from possible 3 for 2 marks*	2

ANSWERS TO HIGHER FOR CfE GERMAN

Question		Expected Answer(s)	Max mark
1	d	• The government/seat of government is there • Full of history • Multi-cultural city • Lots of art galleries and museums • Can see the remnants of the (Berlin) Wall *Any 1 point from possible 5 for 1 mark*	1
1	e	• To improve their German • Academic institutions are recognised worldwide • Qualifications are recognized worldwide *Any 1 point from possible 3 for 1 mark*	1
1	f	• The report highlights why many tourists and students come to Germany	1

Item 2

Question			Expected Answer(s)	Max mark
2	a	i	• The day before yesterday	1
2		ii	• In the south-west (in a small town)	1
2	b		• He was homesick • He didn't understand everything • The family spoke too quickly • They had a (strong) accent • They were patient with him *Any 1 point from possible 5 for 1 mark*	2
2	c		• He shared a room with his host brother • They have similar interests • They were in the same class at school • They could do homework together *Any 2 points from possible 4 for 2 marks*	2
2	d	i	• All the pupils were interested in him • He spoke a lot about Scotland (especially in the English class) • He was the centre of attention in the English classes/lessons *Any 1 point from possible 3 for 1 mark*	1
2		ii	• They have lots of free time/many hobbies • There are few free-time activities offered at school • Many pupils are in clubs *Any 1 point from possible 3 for 1 mark*	1
2	e		• The shops were closed on a Sunday • He had more time to spend with the family • He often went hillwalking • He often went to a lake to swim and windsurf • The views were breathtaking/the air was fresh *Any 2 points from possible 5 for 2 marks*	2

Question			Expected Answer(s)	Max mark
2	f	i	• His German improved • He got an insight into German (daily) life • He became more confident • He met new friends *Any 2 points from possible 4 for 2 marks*	2
2		ii	• To study foreign languages at university • To spend another year abroad *Any 1 point from possible 2 for 1 mark*	1

Section 1 – Writing

Please see p145–147 for General Marking Principles for Higher German Writing.

HIGHER FOR CfE GERMAN MODEL PAPER 2

Reading

Question		Expected Answer(s)	Max mark
1		• Trouble/fights • Quite a lot of pressure from parents	2
2	a	• They were disappointed • They blamed him • They cancelled his football *Any 2 points from possible 3 for 2 marks*	2
	b	• It's the only thing/area he is successful at outside of school • It's not motivating/it is anything but motivating • Motivation is the key to success	3
3		• Some are angry and blame the teachers • Some want to know how they can help • For some parents, it does not seem important *Any 2 points from possible 3 for 2 marks*	2
4		• Concentrate on the future • Think over together with the child what they can do • Parents can ask their child "How can we help you?" • Do not plan the whole year in advance • A whole year is too long and not appropriate • Parents should become interested in their child's progress • Parents should motivate and spur on their child • Set realistic goals which are achievable *Any 3 points from possible 8 for 3 marks*	3
5	a	• Rewards should be social, not material	1
	b	• Go to the cinema • Go on an excursion • Camping with parents at the weekend *Any 2 points from possible 3 for 2 marks*	2
6		• Take (a degree) of responsibility for their grades • Actively seek help • Develop learning strategies • Find own learning rhythm • Study at the same time every day *Any 2 points from possible 5 for 2 marks*	2
7		• School problems should be solved at school. Holidays are for the holidays.	1

Question		Expected Answer(s)	Max mark
8		Outline of possible answers: The author has a **negative view** on school reports for the following reasons: • He states that school reports do not reflect the effort that pupils have put in • He states that school reports can cause a lot of problems at home • He states that school reports can have an impact on pupils' hobbies and spare time activities The author has a **positive view** on school reports for the following reasons: • He states that pupils learn to be (more) responsible for their reports and grades • He states that pupils are encouraged to become more organised in their school work and in their learning The author has a **mixed view** on school reports for the following reasons: • He states that school reports can cause a lot of problems at home but they can also encourage pupils to become more responsible for their own learning	2
9	1	• Not all subjects are important in the eyes of parents	2
	2	• says English teacher Kai Jones. They do not experience/know	2
	3	• whether their child has made an effort	2
	4	• invested time, learned vocabulary	2
	5	• and done his/her homework.	2

Directed Writing

Please refer back to p142–144 for further advice on the General Marking Principles for Higher German Directed Writing.

Section 1 – Listening

Item 1

Question		Expected Answer(s)	Max mark
1	a	• Almost 90% of young people have a mobile phone and internet access • Three quarters have a smartphone *Any 1 point from possible 2 for 1 mark*	1
1	b	• Many parents cannot afford the latest/newest devices • Young people can no longer concentrate • They spend less time with their friends face-to-face *Any 2 points from possible 3 for 2 marks*	2
1	c	• Young people can keep in contact with family and friends • They can find out information quickly	2

ANSWERS TO HIGHER FOR CfE GERMAN

Question			Expected Answer(s)	Max mark
1	d	i	• It can prepare them better for the future • It can support pupils with different learning styles *Any 1 point from possible 2 for 1 mark*	1
1		ii	• It will have a negative effect on pupils' social skills • Pupils can/could film teachers in class *Any 1 point from possible 2 for 1 mark*	1
1	e		• The report highlights some positive and negative impacts of new technology	1

Item 2

Question		Expected Answer(s)	Max mark
2	a	• Last week for her birthday	1
2	b	• To stay in contact with her friends • To download music • To watch online TV • To play (games) *Any 2 points from possible 4 for 2 marks*	2
2	c	• She works part-time in a supermarket • She helps around the house • She vacuums • She walks the dog in the park • She looks after her brother (when her parents go shopping or to the cinema) *Any 2 points from possible 5 for 2 marks*	2
2	d	• She can use the internet when her dad is on the computer • It can save her time • She can check her answers with her friends (if she's stuck) • Her phone has an English dictionary *Any 2 points from possible 4 for 2 marks*	2
2	e	• Some teachers allow phones/not all teachers allow phones • Pupils can use phones at break • Pupils get into trouble if phones go off in class • Phone is confiscated if it goes off in class/phone has to be collected from head teacher if it goes off in class *Any 2 points from possible 4 for 2 marks*	2
2	f	• She left it on a table • It was stolen • She lost all her numbers and photos • She was really upset *Any 2 points from possible 4 for 2 marks*	2
2	g	• Going to visit her gran in the country(side) • Going for a walk in the woods • Meeting her (boy)friend in town (on Sunday) *Any 1 point from possible 3 for 1 mark*	1

Section 2 — Writing

Please see p145–147 for General Marking Principles for Higher German Writing.

HIGHER FOR CfE GERMAN MODEL PAPER 3

Reading

Question			Expected Answer(s)	
1			• Branded clothes • Driving licence • Holiday with friends *Any 2 points from possible 3 for 2 marks*	2
2			• Job adverts in the newspaper • Friends and family may know companies who are hiring • Noticeboards in supermarkets *Any 2 points from possible 3 for 2 marks*	2
3			• The demand for jobs is high • There are more people applying than jobs • There is competition from people doing mini-jobs • People are applying who already have experience • Low mobility of pupils *Any 2 points from possible 5 for 2 marks*	2
4	a		• They are (usually) available longer • There are fewer working conditions	2
	b		• Stack shelves	1
5	a		• The ability to to increase their pocket money • The ability to fulfil a special request • The ability to buy a new games console or a new smartphone *Any 2 points from possible 3 for 2 marks*	2
	b		• They can buy something that their parents do not want to pay for • They can buy something that their parents cannot afford *Any 1 point from possible 2 for 1 mark*	1
6			• First impressions/experience of the world of work • Increased chances of a training place • Employer is happy to see pupils applying who have work experience *Any 2 points from possible 3 for 2 marks*	2
7	a		• Contact with customers • More responsibility *Any 1 point from possible 2 for 1 mark*	1
	b		• She is exhausted after a long day at work • Her boyfriend is annoyed because he does not see her often *Any 1 point from possible 2 for 1 mark*	1
	c		• Do a world tour • Go to college • Study business studies *Any 1 point from possible 3 for 1 mark*	1

Question			Expected Answer(s)	Max mark
8			• You need to have time for yourself • You need to watch you do not get exploited *Any 1 point from possible 2 for 1 mark*	1
9			Outline of possible answers: The writer is **positive** about holiday jobs for the following reasons: • He states that holiday jobs are good for pupils as they can earn pocket money and develop skills • He states that it gives them the opportunity to experience the world of work and may help to get a job in the future The writer is **negative** about holiday jobs for the following reasons: • He states that part-time jobs can have a negative effect on school work as pupils are tired and have less time to do homework • He also states that part-time jobs take away time for relaxation and hobbies	2
10	1		• Even going window-shopping in the city centre can help.	2
	2		• Ice-cream parlours, cafes, restaurants and many other small shops	2
	3		• are looking for temporary workers	2
	4		• especially in the summer holidays who can do easy tasks	2
	5		• for which no previous knowledge is necessary.	2

Directed Writing

Please refer back to p142–144 for further advice on the General Marking Principles for Higher German Directed Writing.

Section 1 – Listening

Item 1

Question		Expected Answer(s)	Max mark
1	a	• ¼ of pupils/every fourth pupil go to (one of the 281) all-day schools • 8 years ago, it was one in 10 *Any 1 point from possible 2 for 1 mark*	1
1	b	• More choice of subjects (art and PE) • Pupils get help with their homework (in the afternoon) • Pupils get the opportunity to work together • There is a personal timetable for each pupil • (Working) parents do not need to worry about childcare and lunch *Any 2 points from possible 5 for 2 marks*	2
1	c	• Higher costs for material and teachers • Less free time (for hobbies, music school and clubs) • Teachers have more influence on upbringing • Pupils are tired after a long day at school *Any 2 points from possible 4 for 2 marks*	2
1	d	• A good timetable • A timetable that is not too much for pupils • A balanced timetable/a timetable with a mix of learning and relaxing *Any 2 points from possible 3 for 2 marks*	2
1	e	• The report highlights that the government is positive about all day schools	1

Item 2

Question			Expected Answer(s)	Max mark
2	a	i	• A maths test (tomorrow)	1
		ii	• She does not want to disappoint her parents • There is performance pressure (from her parents) • Her older sister got good grades (in the Abitur) (2 years ago) *Any 2 points from possible 3 for 2 marks*	2
2	b		• She feels guilty • She should be using every minute to study *Any 1 point from possible 2 for 1 mark*	1
2	c	i	• It's her favourite subject it's extremely interesting • The teacher is great at teaching/explaining things • She remembers everything easily *Any 2 points from possible 3 for 2 marks*	2
2		ii	• She can't stand it • The teacher is monotonous • She does not understand the teacher's explanation • It's repetitive *Any 2 points from possible 4 for 2 marks*	2
2	d		• She sticks notes and pictures to the wall • She drinks lots of water • She does sport *Any 1 point from possible 3 for 1 mark*	1
2	e	i	• She wants to become a chemist	1
2		ii	• 5 years at university • A one-year work experience • State exams • Learn continually – new medicine every year *Any 2 points from possible 4 for 2 marks*	2

Section 2 – Writing

Please see p145–147 for General Marking Principles for Higher German Writing.

… ANSWERS TO HIGHER FOR CfE GERMAN 153

HIGHER FOR CfE GERMAN
MODEL PAPER 4

Reading

Question		Expected Answer(s)	Max mark
1		• To experience something new • To find friends from all over the world • To be part of a (foreign) family *Any 2 points from possible 3 for 2 marks*	2
2		• The famous/well-known (Scottish) humour • The typical (Scottish) way of life	2
3	a	• Cars drive on the other left-hand side • Getting in the car on the German driver's side as a passenger *Any 1 point from possible 2 for 1 mark*	1
	b	• She thought people drank tea and ate cakes at 5pm • It's a nutritious warm meal • Because they only eat a packed lunch in the afternoon *Any 2 points from possible 3 for 2 marks*	2
4	a	• It was shorter than she thought it was going to be • It was like a holiday	2
	b	• Psychology • Travel • Tourism *Any 2 points from possible 3 for 1 mark*	1
	c	• Wide/interesting choice • The decision/deciding was difficult *Any 1 point from possible 2 for 1 mark1*	1
5	a	• She had to go to another school in town	1
	b	• She got the opportunity to meet new friends	1
6	a	• After an unforgettable Christmas time • After an exciting Hogmanay with the family • After a night at the cinema and going out for pizza with her best friend *Any 2 points from possible 3 for 2 marks*	2
	b	• She was upset/tears were shed • Her time in Scotland was too short • She is keen/planning to return *Any 2 points from possible 3 for 2 marks*	2
7		• She learnt lots about Scottish life • She overcame lots of clichés • It was a country different to what she imagined *Any 1 point from possible 3 for 1 mark*	1
8		Outline of possible answers: The writer's experience was generally positive for the following reasons: • She would like to return • She says it changed her perceptions • She uses lots of positive language • She includes very few negative points	2

Question		Expected Answer(s)	Max mark
9	1	• I do not regret my decision one bit/at all	2
	2	• to have left/leave Germany for a while.	2
	3	• It was a great experience, I found a second home in Edinburgh	2
	4	• Re-orientating yourself takes time,	2
	5	• but it's worth it.	2

Directed Writing

Please refer back to p142–144 for further advice on the General Marking Principles for Higher German Directed Writing.

Section 1 – Listening

Item 1

Question		Expected Answer(s)	Max mark
1	a	• 1/10 pupils work alongside school • ½ (50%) work during the summer holidays *Any 1 point from possible 2 for 1 mark*	1
1	b	i • 2 hours a day	1
		ii • Walking dogs • Giving tuition • Delivering newspapers • Gardening *Any 2 points from possible 4 for 2 marks*	2
1	c	• To learn to handle money/financial responsibility • To understand the value of money • To get an insight into the world of work • To gain new qualities (punctuality, organisation and confidence) *Any 2 points from possible 4 for 2 marks*	2
1	d	• Voluntary work • It must not have an negative impact on school work *Any 1 point from possible 2 for 1 mark*	1
1	e	• The report is mostly positive about the impact of part-time work	1

Item 2

Question		Expected Answer(s)	Max mark
2	a	i • In a small Italian restaurant in the town centre (across from the bank)	1
		ii • A year and a half	1
2	b	• He had to fill out an application form online • He sent in his CV • He attended an interview • He had to do a four-week trial and training *Any 2 points from possible 4 for 2 marks*	2

Question			Expected Answer(s)	Max mark
2	c		• Take customers' orders • Answer customers' queries/questions • Put the order into the computer • Prepare and serve the drinks • Handle money/settle the bill • Prepare the table for the next guests *Any 2 points from possible 6 for 2 marks*	2
2	d		• Time flies when you are busy • He's tired in the morning at school • His teachers complain if he hasn't done his homework • The pay is quite good for young people • He's allowed to keep his tips *Any 2 points from possible 5 for 2 marks*	2
2	e		• He gets on quite well with them • There are sometimes rows • [Which is] normal when you work under pressure • It's important to work as a team *Any 2 points from possible 4 for 2 marks*	2
2	f	i	• He doesn't get pocket money • His parents buy him what he needs *Any 1 point from possible 2 for 1 mark*	1
		ii	• He thinks it's fair • He's independent • He can spend his money on what he wants *Any 1 point from possible 3 for 1 mark*	1

Section 2 — Writing

Please see p145—147 for General Marking Principles for Higher German Writing.

Acknowledgements

Hodder Gibson would like to thank SQA for use of any past exam questions that may have been used in model papers, whether amended or in original form.